An Introduction to
Statutory Interpretation
and the Legislative Process

D0208698

EDITORIAL ADVISORY BOARD
Aspen Publishers
Law and Business Education

Richard A. Epstein
James Parker Hall Distinguished Service Professor of Law
University of Chicago

E. Allan Farnsworth
Alfred McCormack Professor of Law
Columbia University

Ronald J. Gilson
Charles J. Meyers Professor of Law and Business
Stanford University
Marc and Eva Stern Professor of Law and Business
Columbia University

Geoffrey C. Hazard, Jr.
Trustee Professor of Law
University of Pennsylvania

James E. Krier
Earl Warren DeLano Professor of Law
University of Michigan

Elizabeth Warren
Leo Gottlieb Professor of Law
Harvard University

Bernard Wolfman
Fessenden Professor of Law
Harvard University

An Introduction to Statutory Interpretation and the Legislative Process

Abner J. Mikva

Visiting Professor of Law and Walter V. Schaefer Scholar
University of Chicago Law School

Eric Lane

Eric J. Schmertz Distinguished Professor of
Public Law and Public Service
Hofstra University School of Law

Aspen Law & Business
A Division of Aspen Publishers, Inc.

Copyright © 1997 by Abner J. Mikva and Eric Lane

All rights reserved. No part of this publication may be reproduced or transmitted in any form or by any means, electronic or mechanical, including photocopy, recording, or any information storage and retrieval system, without permission in writing from the publisher. Requests for permission to make copies of any part of this publication should be mailed to:

Permissions
Aspen Law & Business
1185 Avenue of the Americas
New York, NY 10036

Printed in the United States of America

Library of Congress Cataloging-in-Publication Data

Mikva, Abner J.
    An introduction to statutory interpretation and the legislative process / Abner J. Mikva, Eric Lane.
       p. cm.
    Includes bibliographical references and index.
    ISBN 1-56706-612-7 (pbk.)
       1. Law — United States — Interpretation and construction.
2. Legislation — United States.   I. Lane, Eric, 1943- .
II. Title.
KF425.M55 1997
348.73'22 — dc21
                                  97-23133
                                      CIP

To the new young people who have become so much a part of my life — my grandchildren. I hope that the legislative process works even better to serve the needs of their generation.

— Abner J. Mikva

To a wise and gentle man, Burton C. Agata, my teacher and friend, without whom I would never have become a law school professor or written this book.

To my wife, Joyce Talmadge, who gives special meaning to everything I do.

— Eric Lane

Summary of Contents

Contents

Chapter Two
The Legislative Process 57

Chapter Three
The Enactment of a Statute 101

Chapter Four
The Anatomy of a Statute   **143**

Chapter Five
The Publication of Statutes   **175**

Conclusion   *189*

Foreword

To understand the law, one must understand the legislative process. The authors combine a legislator's first-hand knowledge, with a judge's practical wisdom and a teacher's communicative skills, to explain to the student, to the practitioner, and to the general reader just how that process works. This book should help to bring about better legal argument and better statutory interpretation. It is essential reading for all who have an interest in the law.

Justice Stephen Breyer

June 1997

Introduction

This book is for students of the law who need a better understanding of statutes: the methods and theories of their interpretation; the processes and steps for their enactment, the conventions for their drafting, and the manner in which they are published and used by lawyers and the courts.

We live in an age of statutes in which the nation's legislatures serve actively as the dominant institutions for determining public policy and translating it into law. Through statutes, today's legislatures:

- redistribute enormous amounts of wealth for the benefit of the poor, the ill, the aged, the unemployed, and the disabled, to name a few, but also, sometimes, for the benefit of very narrow interests, which gain legislative favor through various means;
- regulate the market by prohibiting trusts, requiring minimum wages, controlling wages and prices, setting trade policy, favoring certain interests through tax incentives, setting the borrowing limit, and authorizing huge expenditures;
- regulate the health and safety of workers;
- regulate labor relations;
- support huge transportation systems;
- maintain and ultimately govern school systems;
- regulate the environment;
- address race, sex, disability, and age discrimination in the political process and in the workplace;
- regulate risk in consumer products;
- require fairness and reduce commercialization in broadcasting;
- define property rights;
- create standards of acceptable individual behavior;
- define and regulate familial relations; and

- where appropriate, create administrative agencies and authorize the expenditure of enormous amounts of money for the administration of programs.

For the student of law, the ascendancy of statutes has required a reshaping of the traditional law practice and the traditional law school curriculum. The questions lawyers now are asked to answer and to litigate very frequently revolve around the interpretation of statutes. Lawyers must also be aware of statutory development in the same manner that they must be aware of case development. A client's interests are not well served by a lawyer who does not keep abreast of imminent or potential changes in relevant laws.

This effort to follow the statutory landscape requires a facility with the tools of legislative research, such as the committee reports, the Congressional Record, other legislatively generated materials, and various privately produced print and electronic services. More difficult, this task requires the researcher to understand the information provided by these services. Information that proposed legislation (a bill) in a particular legislative substantive committee, in the House Committee on Rules, or in a conference committee only reports a bill's location. A lawyer advising a client on the status of a particular bill must be able to give meaning to this information. He or she must be able to comment on the likelihood of the bill's movement, the possibility of amendment, and on the numerous other factors that allow a client to fully understand the status of proposed legislation. Also, a part of a lawyer's function may be to represent a client's interest before the legislature, through lobbying legislators, preparing testimony for legislative committees, or appearing before them. Finally, the modern practitioner must be able to draft legislation with the same facility as he or she drafts transactional or litigation documents.

Statutory ascendancy has also affected the law school curriculum. A number of law schools have adopted courses on the legislative process or parts of it, usually with some emphasis on statutory interpretation and some research and writing courses now have statutory drafting components. But the greatest impact has revealed itself in the rising overall number of statutory courses, now offered as part of the law school curriculum. As legislatures have enacted the broad array of statutory programs that demark the age of statutes, law schools have followed suit by adopting courses that study the application of these statutes, aided by the increasing number of case books on such subjects. Examples are courses on antitrust, social welfare, civil rights, workers' rights, consumers' rights, and environmental legislation.

Equally as significant is the number of statutes that have replaced the common law as a basis for the traditional courses in law. For example, courses and texts on contracts must deal with the Uniform Commercial Code; courses and texts on torts must reflect legislative attempts to regulate product liability. And courses and texts on property usually address at least the Federal Fair Housing Act.

Despite this attention to statutory law, statutory law courses do not, as a rule, explore the interpretive or legislative process. Their attention is usually on the judicial application of a particular statute to a particular case and sometimes on the policy issues that a particular decision might raise. Omitted from such a focus is any broader look at the methodologies and theories employed by the courts to apply statutes, the processes through which statutes are enacted, the forces that influence their ultimate content, or the various conventions used in the drafting of a statute, which are important to its understanding and implementation. As Judge Richard Posner has so aptly stated:

> Most teachers of statutory fields believe that they have only enough time to introduce the students to the field. . . . They do not feel they have enough time to explore with the class the process by which the legislation is enacted, the political and economic forces that shaped it, or even the methods the courts use to interpret it, as distinct from the particular interpretation that courts have made.

Richard A. Posner, Statutory Interpretation — In the Classroom and in the Courtroom, 50 U. Chi. L. Rev. 800, 802 (1983).

The book addresses the issue raised by Judge Posner and more broadly attempts, in a single volume, to provide students of the law with access to the related processes of statutory interpretation and enactment. The book is divided into five chapters. Chapter One is a primer on statutory interpretation.

Included is a discussion of judicial approaches to statutory interpretation and the tools employed for that purpose (for example, legislative history, canons of interpretation, and agency interpretations). Also discussed are traditional and recent criticisms of such approaches and the use of such tools. The chapter is loosely organized around two types of cases: ones in which the statutory language is clear and should resolve the issue before the court, and ones in which the statutory language is unclear so that the court must search for its meaning elsewhere. We adopt such an organization because we believe it is the best way to also demonstrate that statutory interpretation is not simply the search for legislative meaning or intent, but also the exercise of power by a separate branch of government. We start with the chapter on statutory interpretation, recognizing that it might be more logical to place this chapter after our chapters on the legislative process. Indeed, our textbook uses that organizational design, Abner J. Mikva and Eric Lane, Legislative Process (1995). Our view, in this case, is that statutory interpretation should come first because it is through the experience of reading interpretive cases that most students will reach this book. But the remaining chapters each stand on their own, and nothing limits the instructor or reader from changing the order in which they are read. For example, Professor Lane uses the text as part of his material in a first-year course on lawmaking institutions and starts with the procedural chapters.

Chapters Two and Three introduce the legislative process. Chapter Two addresses the environment in which the consideration of legislation takes place. For some readers (those, for example, with political science backgrounds), parts of this chapter will be familiar. But in our experience this educational background is not as universal as might be thought. Even for those with such a background, the chapter provides a good review and some different insights into the dynamics of the enactment process. Chapter Three is unique. Its goal is to provide a basic understanding of the details and language of the legislative process by following a particular bill through the window of the Congressional Record and then by discussing more generally what is happening.

Chapters Four and Five focus on statutes themselves and their publication. In Chapter Four, the subject is the anatomy of statutes, their structure, form, and generic provisions. Finally, we end with a short Chapter Five. This chapter includes information that most students and many lawyers know little about. For example, most students consider all codes to be the law rather than prima facie evidence of the law, subject to rebuttal by statutes at large or session laws.

In our presentation we frequently, but not exclusively, focus on federal statutes, federal courts, and congressional practices. This is not intended to diminish the significant role of state courts or state legislatures in the interpretation or enactment of legislation. Indeed, state courts and legislatures are far more active interpreters and enactors of statutes. Rather, it is our view that the similarities between the federal and state processes far overshadow their differences and that attention to the federal processes, with appropriate references to state processes, will serve to introduce students of law to all of the varieties of the nation's interpretive and enactment processes.

A.J.M.
E.L.

June 1997

Acknowledgments

We happily acknowledge the efforts of many who have contributed to this project. First, Dean Stuart Rabinowitz of the Hofstra University School of Law has, as ever, been extremely generous in his support of this effort. Second, a number of Hofstra Law School students have performed yeomen services as research assistants, commentators, and editors. They include Alan Barr, Catherine Carney, Stephan Cirami, Lisa Gunder, Mary Jewels, Barbara O'Connor, Jacqueline Sobotta, and Elaine Sammon. Third, Roz Weiss, Professor Lane's secretary, again supplied the support necessary to coordinate this effort. Fourth, numerous colleagues in academia and in government, too many to list, consulted with us on ideas and provided helpful counsel. Fifth, David Gross at Budd Larner Gross Rosenbaum Greenberg & Sade provided keen insights into how practicing lawyers view and use statutes, and former New Jersey Appellate Judge Geoffrey Gaulkin, now of the Budd Larner firm, sharpened our views of how judges read them. Finally, Carol McGeehan and other members of the Aspen team offered us the opportunity to introduce a new type of book to their impressive catalogue of titles. Also the comments of anonymous faculty reviewers supplied to us through the Aspen efforts provided invaluable guidance and commentary to the final shape of this work, and Lisa Wehrle once again made sense of our work through her excellent copyediting. To all, thanks.

About the Authors

ABNER J. MIKVA

Abner J. Mikva is currently Visiting Professor of Law and the Walter V. Schaefer Scholar at the University of Chicago Law School. Prior to his professorship, he served as Counsel to the President of the United States, as judge on the United States Court of Appeals for the District of Columbia Circuit, and as its chief judge from January 1991 to September 1994. Before coming to the bench, he served as a Congressman for five terms and, prior to that, as a member of the Illinois House of Representatives. He also served as a law clerk to Supreme Court Justice Sherman Minton.

ERIC LANE

Eric Lane is the Eric J. Schmertz Distinguished Professor of Public Law and Public Service at Hofstra University School of Law, where he has been teaching since 1976. During this period, he has also served as Counsel to the New York State Temporary Commission on Constitutional Revision (1993-1995), as Chair of the New York City Task Force on Charter Implementation (1990), as Executive Director/Counsel to the New York City Charter Revision Commission (1986-1989), and as Chief Counsel to the New York State Senate Minority (1981-1986).

CHAPTER ONE_____

The Interpretation of Statutes

In this chapter, we offer a brief primer on the judicial interpretation of statutes. We begin with a definition of the term *statute*, move to a discussion of how courts interpret clear and unclear statutes, take a look at some modern theories of interpretation, and finally, offer an introductory discussion of judicial approaches to the interpretation of statutes enacted through initiative and referendum.

A. WHAT IS A STATUTE?

The end product of the legislative process is a *statute* (also referred to as an *act* or *legislation*). On their face, statutes appear abstract. They reveal no story, no characters, no drama — usually just a dry recitation of rights and obligations. Sometimes their provisions conflict or are unclear or vague. But two thoughts ought to be borne in mind about statutes. First, statutes never represent the abstract exercise of power. They are always the legislative response to problems identified by legislative bodies as needing resolution in a particular fashion. Every statute has a story behind it, although (unlike a judicial decision) its story is usually untold in the statutory language. Often the story is quite dramatic. Second, statutes are almost always the products of compromise. For a statute to be enacted, it must receive the support of at least a majority of the members of each legislative house and a supermajority in the case of executive veto. This level of consensus is extremely difficult to achieve, even among members of the same political party. Americans possess different and often competing views about the nature of problems that government ought to resolve and the substance of such resolution. Legislators reflect these differing ideas about the nature of particular problems and about their resolution. For a bill to go forward in this environment, compromise is required. Some compromises result in a proposed provision being omitted from a statute, some result in changes in existing language, some result in additional (sometimes redundant, sometimes conflicting) language or provisions, and some result in clear statutory language purposely being made unclear. At each step of this compromise process proponents of the existing legislation must decide whether the legislative benefit is worth the compromise cost.

A statute is also a command of a particular legislature (federal, state, municipal) that must be obeyed, under threat of governmental sanction, by those whose behavior it regulates. For a member of the public, the question then is whether a statute regulates particular behavior. Answering this question usually is not difficult because the meaning of the statute in the context of the particular behavior is clear. Statutes are written in English and generally use terms that carry common meanings or contain definitions of terms. For example, some state penal codes provide that

> A person is guilty of theft if he unlawfully takes, or exercises unlawful control over, movable property of another with purpose to deprive him thereof.

While the language of this provision is perhaps technical, its application would be clear to most people in most instances. Even terms that are somewhat less than common to laypeople are frequently understood by the parties under the statute's ambit. All of this is to mark the obvious, but sometimes overlooked, point that statutes are overwhelmingly interpreted and implemented informally, that is, without invoking the formal processes of administrative agencies or the courts.

This, of course, is not always the case. In the age of statutes, their interpretation constitutes a major part of the judicial function. This is evidenced by federal and state appellate court dockets that are filled with cases emanating from disputes over the meaning of statutory language, in the context of a particular fact pattern. It is also evidenced by the attention of law school curricula to the interpretation of statutes. These disputes arise, for the most part, because statutory provisions do not provide clear answers to questions concerning particular behavior. As Justice, then Judge, Antonin Scalia observed during the hearing for his nomination to the Supreme Court, "we do not normally have a lawsuit in front of us if the language of a statute is clear." Hearings before the Senate Comm. on the Judiciary, 99th Cong., 2d Sess. 65 (Aug. 5-6, 1986).

Once such a case is before the court, lawyers must argue why the statute covers or does not cover the behavior in question, and judges must "find the meaning" of the statute to decide whether it regulates the particular conduct at issue. It is this search for "meaning" that constitutes judicial interpretation. Sometimes, even when the language of a statute is clear with respect to a particular fact pattern, courts will still conduct a "search for its meaning" because they do not believe that the application of clear language results in the outcome the legislature intended or, in fewer cases, because of some preference they have for an outcome different from that imposed by the statute's language. The willingness of courts to ignore a particular statute's plain meaning in certain instances is an important part of any study of statutory interpretation and is integral to an understanding of the history of statutory interpretation and the theoretical debates that continue to swirl about this important judicial function. An awareness of such potential judicial action is also important to the lawyer who must advise his or her client on how a particular statute applies to particular behavior. Such awareness should lead not to a conclusion that the statutory construction is a random judicial function but only to a more contextual and historical look at statutory interpretation and a more careful study of the approaches of individual judges to statutory interpretation. In this chapter, we will discuss the judicial approaches to statutory interpretation, provide some historical and theoretical context for their exercise, and explore some of the modern theoretical debates that surround the exercise of this judicial function.

We offer one last introductory note. In the discussion of statutory interpretation, we do not distinguish between federal and state decisions and use both. In our view, approaches to statutory interpretation are not divisible into "state" and "federal." Differences in interpretive approaches are the product of individual judicial sensibilities and not, for the most part, particular jurisdictions. Two differences do emerge: the frequency with which state courts rely on canons of construction (see section B3a of this chapter) and the number of "showdown" questions (see section B4 of this chapter) that state courts confront. These differences between federal and state courts are not a consequence of different approaches to statutory construction but a result of the slimness and inaccessibility of state legislative histories, which leave state courts with little guidance in the case of unclear statutes. Also, some states do have statutes that contain interpretive rules. While for the most part they deal with minor interpretive issues (*he* means *he or she*), sometimes they are more substantive.

B. HOW JUDGES INTERPRET STATUTES

All judicial approaches to statutory interpretation are framed by the constitutional truism that the judicial will must bend to the legislative command. It is through the subordination of the judiciary to the legislature that our laws are assured their "democratic pedigree." Cass R. Sunstein, After the Rights Revolution 113 (1990). More starkly stated by Judge Posner, a statute is "a command issued by a superior body (the legislature) to a subordinate body (the judiciary)." Richard A. Posner, The Problems of Jurisprudence 265 (1990).

Such legislative superiority means that, in the application of statutes, judges are not free to resolve a dispute by simply imposing their outcome preferences, as they might do in a common law setting, or to treat statutory laws as loosely binding precedents, as they might treat common law precedents. Rather, they must follow the legislative command by applying the statute's language or referring to legislative intent or purpose as discerned through legislative history or canons of construction. As Judge Patricia Wald has written:

> Personal experience has revealed that the nearly universal view among federal judges is that when we are called upon to interpret statutes, it is our primary responsibility, within constitutional limits, to subordinate our wishes to the will of Congress

because the legislators' collective intention, however discerned, trumps the will of the court.

Patricia M. Wald, The Sizzling Sleeper: The Use of Legislative History in Construing Statutes in the 1988-89 Term of the United States Supreme Court, 39 Am. U. L. Rev. 277, 281 (1990).

Judge Wald's rendition of legislative supremacy may catch an uninitiated reader off-guard because of the normal assumption that the "will" of a legislative body would be found in a statute's text. As noted earlier, often it is, but, as we also noted, sometimes the text is unclear in the context of a particular fact pattern, and a statute's meaning must be drawn from other sources. But the existence of unclear statutes does not alone explain Wald's reference to "legislators' collective intention, *however discerned*." Rather, her observation also frames a historical and continuing debate over what Judge Richard Posner has characterized as "the important question concerning statutory interpretation, which is political rather than epistemic: how free *should* judges feel themselves to be from the fetters of text and legislative intent in applying statutes." Richard A. Posner, The Problems of Jurisprudence 271 (1990). The question is not only what the legislature meant by a certain statutory provision in the context of a particular fact pattern, but also how to square such legislative meaning with a judicial preference for what a decision should be. This is what one observer has characterized as the "tension between literal and non-literal interpretations" of statutes. William S. Blatt, The History of Statutory Interpretation: A Study in Form and Substance, 6 Cardozo L. Rev. 799, 811 (1985).

On reflection, the existence of judicial outcome preferences should come as no surprise. Judges are not automatons. They have policy preferences and form outcome preferences in particular cases. These preferences are sometimes so compelling that a judge may want to impose them as the law in a particular case despite statutory language to the contrary or evidence of statutory meaning to the contrary. As Justice Holmes wrote:

> The language of judicial decision is mainly the language of logic. And the logical method and form flatter that longing for certainty and for repose which is in every human mind. But certainty generally is illusion, and repose is not the destiny of man.

Behind the logical form lies a judgment as to the relative worth
and importance of competing legislative rounds, often an inar-
ticulate and unconscious judgment, it is true, and yet the very
root and nerve of the whole proceeding.

Oliver W. Holmes, The Path of the Law, 10 Harv. L. Rev. 457,
468-469 (1897). Whether a judge follows such a course and imposes his or her own preference in a particular case depends
on a number of factors, including the intensity of the preference, the clarity of the contrary statute's meaning, and his or
her view of the obligation to obey statutory commands. A
judge may have a strong preference that he or she does not
impose because the statute, either through its language or its
legislative history, commands otherwise. This is probably the
common course taken. In a case in which a judge wants to
impose his or her outcome preference, notwithstanding a
legislative command to the contrary, the judge will not simply
state that he or she is trumping the statute but will argue that
his or her view is consistent with legislative intent or purpose.
This is the larger point Judge Wald is making.

1.   Legislative Meaning, Intent, and Purpose

Statutory interpretation is a search for legislative meaning
in the context of the particular question before the court. If the
statutory language is clearly determinative of the question before the court, the inquiry ends in most instances, because
courts view statutory language as the best evidence of legislative meaning. But sometimes even when the language is clear,
interpreters ask the question, Did the legislature intend the
particular result achieved by applying the statute's plain
meaning to a particular fact pattern? For example, in Tennessee Valley Authority v. Hill, 437 U.S. 153 (1978), the Court
was asked whether a statute that required governmental
agencies to take "such actions necessary to insure that actions
authorized, funded, or carried out by them do not jeopardize
the continued existence of such endangered species" applied
to an almost completed dam and reservoir project for which
many millions of tax dollars had been spent and for which
there were great economic expectations. While the majority
answered the question affirmatively, based on the clear

meaning of the statutory text, the dissenters argued that such an application of the statute was absurd and inconsistent with legislative intent. This case is discussed on page 12.

When a statute is unclear with respect to a particular question, lawyers and courts generally begin their search for statutory meaning by asking the question: Did the legislature intend this particular statutory provision to cover this particular fact pattern? An example of such an inquiry is found in Liparota v. United States, 471 U.S. 419 (1985), a case included or referred to in most criminal law casebooks. In *Liparota*, the defendant was charged with a violation of a federal statute that provided "whoever knowingly uses, transfers, acquires, alters, or possesses coupons or authorization cards [for food stamps] in a manner not authorized by [the statute] or the regulations [of the Department of Agriculture] shall be guilty of a criminal offense." The question for the Court was whether the statute required the defendant to have knowledge of the regulations he was charged with violating or only that he have knowledge of his conduct, that is, that he knowingly acquired the coupons or authorization cards and did not act through ignorance or mistake. The former interpretation would favor the defendant. In reaching its decision, the Court noted: "Although Congress certainly intended by use of the word 'knowingly' to require some mental state with respect to some element of the crime defined in §2024 (b)(1), the interpretations proffered by both parties [knowledge of the regulation or of his conduct] accord with congressional intent to this extent." 471 U.S. at 424. For the Court, the question became how broadly did Congress intend the knowledge requirement to be construed. For reasons we will discuss on pages 23-24, the Court interpreted the statute narrowly, favoring the defendant.

Historically, reference by the courts to legislative intent was the subject of intense critical analysis. Such criticism argued that judges frequently used legislative intent to trump statutory language that the judges disfavor. In other words, if they did not like the outcome effected by the statutory language, they would declare that a favored outcome was required by legislative intent. See, for example, Max Radin, Statutory Interpretation, 43 Harv. L. Rev. 863, 870 (1929-1930). The denial of legislative intent as a reference point for a statutory interpretation left its critics with somewhat of a problem. If reference could not be made to legislative intent, on what basis would a court be able to find the meaning of an unclear statute, or, for some proponents of broader judicial discretion, on what basis would a court be able to exercise discretion beyond the language of a statute? After all, courts still needed to find some legislative peg on which to hang their decision. The response was to refer to a statute's *purpose*, which was seen by its proponents as a more objective standard that is "evident from the thing [statute] itself." Id. at 875. This emphasis on purpose is sometimes referred to as *purposivism*. Purpose, to its proponents, is found by "comparing the new law with the old" and asking "[w]hy would reasonable men, confronted with the law as it was, have enacted this new law to replace it?" Henry Hart and Albert Sacks, The Legal Process: Basic Problems in the Making and Application of Law 1415 (10th ed. 1958). For an example of a case in which the Supreme Court focuses on purpose to the exclusion of clear statutory language, see United Steelworkers of America, AFL-CIO-CLC v. Weber, 443 U.S. 193 (1979), discussed on pages 14-16.

Whether or not a real distinction exists between legislative *intent* or *purpose*, other than that made in historical context, courts have basically ignored this debate in their search for statutory meaning. Courts often use *intent* unanalytically and interchangeably with *purpose* to refer to a source of statutory meaning (the intent of the legislature, the purpose of the legislation) outside of the language of the statute at issue in the litigation. For example, in one paragraph in *Liparota*, the Court states "the interpretations proffered by both . . . accord with congressional intent. . . . The legislative history . . . contains nothing that would clarify the Congressional purpose on this point." 471 U.S. at 424-425. It is in this interchangeable way that we use the term.

One cautionary note: Sometimes a statement of legislative purpose is actually enacted into law as a statutory provision. On such occasion, reference to legislative *purpose* and *intent* should not be used interchangeably. *Purpose* should be used to designate the purpose provision, while *intent* should maintain its traditional role as a reference point outside the statute. An example of an enacted purpose clause is taken from the Americans with Disabilities Act of 1990, 42 U.S.C. §§21101 et seq.:

(b) PURPOSE — It is the purpose of this Act —

(1) to provide a clear and comprehensive national mandate for the elimination of discrimination against individuals with disabilities;

(2) to provide clear, strong, consistent, enforceable standards addressing discrimination against individuals with disabilities;

(3) to ensure that the Federal Government plays a central role in enforcing the standards established in this Act on behalf of individuals with disabilities; and

(4) to invoke the sweep of congressional authority, including the power to enforce the fourteenth amendment and to regulate commerce, in order to address the major areas of discrimination faced day-to-day by people with disabilities.

An example of a purpose clause being used in the interpretation of a statute is found in Chapter Four, page 165.

2. *Clear and Unclear Statutory Language*

In our exploration of statutory interpretation, we divide statutes into two categories: those for which the text provides a clear answer to the issue in question and those for which the textual answer is unclear. We make this division because we think that judicial avoidance of a clear legislative command, whether based on a judicial view of legislative intent or on a judicial policy preference, is a unique exercise of judicial power even though the approaches used to "find the legislative meaning" outside the text are the same as those used when the statute is unclear.

a. **The Plain Meaning of a Statute and How It Is Applied: Three Examples**

The starting place for any search for statutory meaning obviously must be the language of the statute in question, for it is the language of a statute that the legislature enacts. As the Supreme Court has written: "It is elementary that the meaning of a statute must, in the first instance, be sought in the language in which the act is framed." Caminetti v. United States,

242 U.S. 470, 485 (1917). If a reading of the statute provides a clear answer to the case (a determination often subject to debate), most judges and commentators would agree, at least in theory, that any inquiry should end because "if that is plain, and if the law is within the constitutional authority of the lawmaking body which passed it, the sole function of the courts is to enforce it according to its terms." Id. at 485. This is known as the *plain meaning rule.*

Cases in which the statutory text provides a plain or clear answer to a dispute generally do not reach the appellate courts, though there are several exceptions to this rule. Sometimes the rigid application of the plain meaning of a statute can lead to absurd results because "[m]eaning depends on context as well as on the semantic and other formal properties of sentences." Richard A. Posner, The Problems of Jurisprudence 269 (1990). As Professor Daniel Farber has written, "For example, virtually no one doubts the correctness of the ancient decision that a statute prohibiting 'letting blood in the streets' did not ban emergency surgery." Daniel A. Farber, Statutory Interpretation and Legislative Supremacy, 78 Geo. L.J. 281, 289 (1989). Applying the literal language in such situations would lead to absurd consequences, ones that constructively could not have been within the purpose of the enacting legislature. This same point can be illustrated by considering a group of students milling around one student's seat during a class break. On entering the classroom, the teacher instructs the students to "sit down immediately." Most people would consider it absurd if the milling students sat down on the floor, rather than returned to their seats. But such exceptions to the plain meaning rule are, largely, theoretical. Rarely is a court faced with clear statutory language that, if applied in a particular case, would be so illogical or contrary to reason (statutory absurdity) that the application constructively could not reflect the will of the enacting legislature.

More typically, a court will choose not to apply a statute's plain language because it judges that such application of the plain language in a particular case is inconsistent with the legislative intent or purpose of the enacting legislature or because it does not agree with the policy outcome dictated by the statute's language. In either case, the court will declare the plain meaning inapplicable as inconsistent with legislative intent or purpose as determined through the application of some canon of interpretation or as evidenced by some piece of legislative history.

Tennessee Valley Authority v. Hill illustrates this point. It is not absurd for the legislature to have wanted to protect endangered species at the cost of stopping a nearly completed project. The dissenters simply disfavored this outcome either because they subjectively thought it was wrong or because, and this may be the same thing, they thought the legislature did not mean this outcome. We underscore, in reference to this traditional exception, the need for relating the decision to legislative intent or purpose. Even if the decision is one based on judicial preference, reference to legislative intent or purpose is necessary to preserve the concept of legislative supremacy and separation of powers.

Three Supreme Court decisions that are often discussed in the literature on statutory interpretation provide examples of the use and avoidance of the plain meaning rule. Each case demonstrates the tension between the application of plain meaning and judicial preferences for different outcomes. Each also demonstrates the rationales used for supporting decisions contrary to the statutory language. We briefly discuss each of these cases below. All italics in the decisional texts are ours, intended to draw attention to the traditional rationale for departing from a statute's plain meaning. In one of these cases, Tennessee Valley Authority v. Hill, 437 U.S. 153 (1978), the Court, over the dissent of three justices, follows the statute's plain meaning. The dissent argues that the application of the statute's clear language is inconsistent with legislative intent. In the other two, Church of the Holy Trinity v. United States, 143 U.S. 457 (1892), and United Steelworkers of America, AFL-CIO-CLC v. Weber, 443 U.S. 193 (1979), the Court departs from the plain statutory language to reach a contrary result. In *Holy Trinity* the departure is based on a judgment that the statute's application would be absurd in the context of the disputed issue, and in *Weber* the majority determined that application of the language in the disputed case would be inconsistent with the statute's purpose. Each of these cases illustrates the historical strains between judicial activism and judicial restraint in statutory interpretation.

Tennessee Valley Authority v. Hill, 437 U.S. 153 (1978).
Tennessee Valley Authority v. Hill is the famous "snail darter"
case. The Endangered Species Act of 1973 required departments of the federal government to take actions "necessary to
insure that actions authorized, funded, or carried out by them
do not jeopardize the continued existence of such endangered
species and threatened species or result in the destruction or
modification of [their] habitat." During the construction of the
huge Tellico Dam and Reservoir Project by the Tennessee Valley Authority, a new species of perch, the three-inch snail
darter, was discovered. After an investigation, the Secretary of
the Interior, pursuant to statutory authority, declared the snail
darter to be an endangered species and the continued construction of the dam project to be a threat to its only known
habitat. For this reason, the Tennessee Valley Authority (TVA)
was required to halt its work on the dam. The TVA protested
this order, particularly because the project was almost completed and many millions of dollars had been expended on the
project. In its challenge, the TVA argued that the halting of an
almost completed project, particularly one of this magnitude,
was not the "intent" of the statute and that such application of
the statute would be "absurd." In ruling against TVA, the
Court wrote:

> One would be hard pressed to find a statutory provision
> whose terms were any plainer than those in §7 of the Endan-
> gered Species Act. . . . Its very words affirmatively command all
> federal agencies *"to insure* that *actions authorized, funded, or
> carried out* by them do not *jeopardize* the continued existence" of
> an endangered species or *"result* in the destruction or
> modification of habitat of such species. . . . "* This language
> admits of no exception.

437 U.S. at 173. The dissent's view in this case provides a good
example of the argument judges make against applying a
statute's plain meaning. "Nor can I believe that Congress
could have *intended* this Act to produce the 'absurd'
result . . . of this case." For a full discussion of this case, see
Abner J. Mikva and Eric Lane, Legislative Process 806-820
(1995).

**Church of the Holy Trinity v. United States, 143 U.S. 457
(1892).** *Holy Trinity* is the most frequently cited authority for

the exercise of judicial discretion in avoidance of the words of a
statute. Its fame lies in its highlighting of the interpretive
canon "It is a familiar rule that a thing may be within the letter
of the statute and yet not within the statute, because not within
its spirit, nor within the intention of its makers." The statute
basically prohibited anyone from bringing foreigners to the
United States "to perform labor or service of any kind" except,
among others, foreigners who were "professional actors, art-
ists, lecturers, or singers." The Church of the Holy Trinity
made a contract with an English pastor, E. Walpole Warren,
pursuant to which he moved to the United States to serve the
church. The dispute before the Court was whether this contract
between the church and Pastor Warren violated the statute.
According to the Court:

> It must be conceded that the act of the corporation is
> within the letter of this section. . . . Not only are the general
> words labor and service both used, but also, as it were to guard
> against any narrow interpretation and emphasize a breadth of
> meaning, to them is added "of any kind"; and, further . . . [the]
> specific exceptions . . . [strengthen] the idea that every other
> kind of labor and service was intended to be reached. . . . While
> there is great force to this reasoning, we cannot think Congress
> *intended* to denounce with penalties a transaction like that in the
> present case. It is a familiar rule, that a thing may be within the
> letter of the statute and yet not within the statute, because not
> within its spirit, nor within the *intention* of its makers. . . . This is
> not the substitution of the will of the judge for that of the
> legislator, for frequently words of a general meaning are used in
> a statute, words broad enough to include an act in question, and
> yet a consideration of the whole legislation, or of the
> circumstances surrounding its enactment, or of the absurd
> results which follow from giving such broad meaning to the
> words, makes it unreasonable to believe that the legislator
> *intended* to include the particular act.

Id. at 458-459. From this point the Court combined references
in legislative committee reports to "manual labor" with its
view of the United States as a "religious nation" to conclude
that the legislation did not intend to prohibit the contract with
Pastor Warren. This was a difficult conclusion to reach in the
face of the statute's language, particularly because of the explicit exception for certain professions among which pastors or

other religious professions were not listed. About this case
Professor Philip Frickey has written:

> In my legislation course, I tell my students that *Holy Trinity
> Church* is the case you always cite when the statutory text is
> hopelessly against you. . . . The tactic of relying upon the case
> does sometimes resemble the "Hail Mary" pass in football. As a
> matter of attorney advocacy, that may be all well and good, but
> as a matter of judicial resolution of a critical social issue, it may
> seem like something altogether different.

Philip P. Frickey, From the Big Sleep to the Big Heat: The Re-
vival of Theory in Statutory Interpretation, 77 Minn. L. Rev.
241, 247 (1992).

**United Steelworkers of America, AFL-CIO-CLC v.
Weber, 443 U.S. 193 (1979).**   The final example of deviation
from statutory plain meaning is a case of far more substantial
social consequence than that of *Church of the Holy Trinity*. It is
one of the cases that form the basis for many affirmative action
programs. The decision has been the subject of considerable
debate, which is described in Abner J. Mikva and Eric Lane,
Legislative Process 835-860 (1995). The dispute in *Weber* is over
the applicability of Title VII of the Civil Rights Act of 1964 to a
contractual arrangement between the United Steelworkers
Union and Kaiser Aluminum & Chemical Corp. "that reserves
for black employees 50% of the openings in an in-plant craft-
training program until the percentage of black craftworkers in
the plant is commensurate with the percentage of blacks in the
local labor force." Title VII of the Civil Rights Act of 1964
prohibited "any employer, labor organization . . . to discrimi-
nate against any individual because of his race, color, religion,
sex, or national origin in admission to, or employment in, any
program established to provide apprenticeship or other
training." Brian Weber, a white employee at one of the Kaiser
plants, had bid for admission to the plant's craft-training
program and was rejected, only because of the affirmative
action arrangement. The dispute before the Court was whether
this rejection constituted racial discrimination. In determining
that it did not, the Court wrote:

Respondent's argument rests upon a *literal interpretation* of . . . the Act. . . .

Respondent's argument is not without force. But it overlooks the significance of the fact that the . . . plan is an affirmative action plan voluntarily adopted by private parties to eliminate traditional patterns of racial segregation. In this context, respondent's reliance upon a literal construction of . . . [the Act] is misplaced. It is [citing *Holy Trinity Church*] a "familiar rule, that a thing may be within the letter of the statute and yet not within the statute, because not within its spirit, nor within the *intentions* of its makers." The prohibition . . . must therefore be read against the background of the *legislative history* of Title VII and the historical context from which the Act arose. Examination of those sources makes clear than an interpretation of the sections that forbade all race-conscious affirmative action would "bring about an end completely at variance with the *purpose* of the statute" and must be rejected.

443 U.S. at 201-202. This purpose, according to the Court, was "to open employment opportunities for Negroes in occupations which have been traditionally closed to them." Stating this purpose does not compel the majority's application of the statute in this case. Prohibiting all discrimination is a remedy consistent with the statute's clear meaning that also satisfies this purpose, albeit more slowly. Both Chief Justice Burger and Justice Rehnquist raise this point in their dissents. According to Chief Justice Burger:

The Court reaches a result I would be inclined to vote for were I a Member of Congress considering a proposed amendment of Title VII. I cannot join the Court's judgment, however, because it is contrary to the explicit language of the statute and arrived at by means wholly incompatible with long-established principles of separation of powers. Under the guise of statutory "construction," the Court effectively rewrites Title VII to achieve what it regards as a desirable result. It "amends" the statute to do precisely what its sponsors and its opponents agreed the statute was not intended to do.

Id. at 216. Much of Justice Rehnquist's decision is an incisive look at the Act's legislative history, which the majority used to support its conclusion but which it never seriously explored. His conclusion from this search was that the legislative history clearly supported the application of the statute's clear meaning that neither blacks nor whites could be discriminated against. This exploration by Justice Rehnquist led to an extremely interesting comment by Justice Blackmun, a member of the decision's majority, concerning the theories of some judges on the application of statutes. This, in our view, is a very straightforward statement of a judge's reasoning for supporting a decision that is contrary to both text and legislative history.

> While I share some of the misgivings expressed in Mr. Justice Rehnquist's dissent concerning the extent to which the legislative history of Title VII clearly supports the result the Court reaches today, I believe that additional considerations practical and equitable, only partially perceived, if perceived at all, by the 88th Congress support the conclusion reached by the Court today.

Id. at 209.

b.   Cases Involving Private Rights of Action and Mistakes

In addition to cases such as those above, two types of cases have often caused tension between the application of a statute's plain meaning and judicial discretion. In one such grouping of cases, courts are asked to create private rights of action in statutes that do not contain them. In the second group, courts are asked to correct what are arguably legislative drafting mistakes.

Adding Private Rights of Action.   The cases dealing with private rights of action have historically involved two questions: (1) whether the legislature intended a private cause of action (sometimes referred to as an implied cause of action), notwithstanding statutory silence, and (2) whether a court, based on the common law practice of providing a remedy for a "wrong," should supply one. The Supreme Court seems to have narrowed the questions to one. "The question of the existence of a statutory cause of action is, of course, one of statutory construction. Our task is limited solely to determining whether Congress intended to create the private right of action." Touche Ross & Co. v. Redington, 442 U.S. 560, 568 (1979). In that case, the statute required broker-dealers to keep and file certain records with the Securities Exchange Commission. Plaintiffs sued Touche Ross, arguing that it had improperly audited and certified the required financial statements of Weis Securities, a bankrupt broker-dealer. Writing for the majority's finding against a private right of action in this case, Justice Rehnquist reasoned:

> Here the statute by its terms grants no private rights to any identifiable class and proscribes no conduct as unlawful. And the parties . . . agree that the legislative history of the 1934 Act does not speak to the issue of private remedies. . . . At least in such a case as this, the inquiry ends there.
>   . . . The ultimate question is one of congressional intent, not one of whether this Court thinks that it can improve upon the statutory scheme that Congress enacted into law.

Id. at 576, 578. For a frequently cited decision in which the Court implied a private right of action, see Cannon v. University of Chicago, 441 U.S. 677 (1979). For a recent exchange on the issue of private rights of action and the basis for their attribution to a statute that does not include them, consider the following exchange between Senator Thurmond and Justice (then nominee) Ruth Bader Ginsburg, taken from the transcripts of Justice Ginsburg's confirmation hearings before the Senate Judiciary Committee. This exchange illustrates that the issue remains a source of concern between the legislature and the judiciary.

> Senator THURMOND: Judge Ginsburg, one very important area of the law is the question of whether courts exceed their authority by creating rights of action for private litigants under Federal statutes where Congress did not expressly provide such rights of action. . . .
> Judge GINSBURG: I think that Congress should express itself plainly on the question of private rights of action. I think that judges would welcome that with great enthusiasm. Judges do not lightly imply private rights of action. In some areas of the law, securities law, for example, where private rights of action have been understood by the courts to be the legislature's intention, and that is always what the court is trying to divine, it appears that the legislature has been content with those im-

plications. It has left them alone now for in some cases even decades.

But I think the judges have said often enough in opinions, we are going to try to find out and try to determine as best we can whether Congress intended there to be a private right of action. We wish that Congress would speak clearly to this question, because, as you said, Senator, the existence of a private right of action or not is for Congress to say.

Dealing with Mistakes.   On occasion, courts determine that a statute contains a drafting error and that its application would be inconsistent with legislative intent or purpose. Often, these cases revolve around questions of punctuation, but may also include other types of errors. The court's task is to decide whether it should provide a correction, despite the statute's clear meaning. Two examples follow. In National Bank of Oregon v. Insurance Agents, 508 U.S. 439 (1993) (a case we will refer to again in Chapter Five), a bank's right to sell insurance in certain circumstances was challenged on the basis of a statute that seemed to prohibit such bank activity. The question for the Court was the location of certain quotation marks that, if read as placed, would have barred the bank from selling insurance. In making its judgment in favor of the bank, the Court reaffirmed a basic judicial approach to the effect of punctuation:

> A statute's plain meaning must be enforced, of course, and the meaning of a statute will typically heed the commands of its punctuation. But a purported plain-meaning analysis based only on punctuation is necessarily incomplete and runs the risk of distorting a statute's true meaning. Along with punctuation, text consists of words living "a communal existence," in the Judge Learned Hand's phrase, the meaning of each word informing the others and "all in their aggregate taking their purport from the setting in which they are used.". . . No more than isolated words or sentences is punctuation alone a reliable guide for discovery of a statute's meaning. . . .
>
> Here, though the deployment of quotation marks . . . points in one direction, all of the other evidence from the statute points the other way. It points so certainly, in our view, as to allow only the conclusion that the punctuation marks were misplaced. . . .

508 U.S. at 455-456.

Errors in punctuation are not the only types of drafting errors courts may confront, although they are perhaps the most frequent ones encountered. In Harris v. Shanahan, 387 P.2d 771 (Kan. 1963), for example, the Kansas Supreme Court was asked to invalidate a legislative districting statute that failed to include a particular Kansas city in any state senate district. In fact, each house of the legislature had passed a bill that had included the missing city within the same legislative district, but this placement erroneously had been dropped by the enrollment clerk. (For an explanation of enrollment, see Chapter 5, section A.) The court declined to add the city to the allotted senate district because the bill presented to and signed by the governor (the enrolled bill that omitted the city) differed from the bill that passed both houses, which did include the city in a particular senate district.

The court might have reached a different decision if the bill that passed the legislature still omitted the particular city but was identical to the bill signed by the governor. In this case a statute would have actually been enacted. If the omission was inadvertent and the legislative record (for example, committee reports) evidenced an intent that the city be located in a particular district, the court might have been willing to insert the city into the district indicated by legislative history, based on its view that "words may be supplied in a statute . . . where omission is due to inadvertence, mistake, accident or clerical error." 387 P.2d at 782.

Some states have statutes that authorize the correction of drafting errors after a bill has been enacted. New Jersey law authorizes their Office of Legislative Services in concurrence with the Attorney General "to correct in the text, but not the title, of any law, such errors in references to other laws and in punctuation and spelling, and other obvious errors in form, which will not affect the substance of the laws." N.J. Stat. Ann. §1:3-1 (West 1992).

c. Applying Unclear Statutes

Most cases of statutory interpretation, especially at the appellate levels, involve language that does not provide courts with clear answers to the question of whether particular conduct is within the statute's reach. In Liparota v. United States, noted on page 7, the Court observed: "[T]he words themselves provide little guidance. Either interpretation would accord with ordinary usage." Several factors account for this. First, words are not perfect symbols for the communication of ideas and may be understood differently by different audiences. Second, and most importantly, while particular events may stimulate the enactment of a statute, statutes are, for the most part, drafted in general terms, addressing *categories* of conduct. No matter how carefully any statute might be drafted, a dispute over its applicability to a particular fact pattern is the natural consequence of its generality. Illustrative of this point is Chisom v. Roemer, 501 U.S. 380 (1991), in which the Supreme Court was asked to decide whether "elected judges" came within the definition of the statutory term "representatives," thereby subjecting the election of judges to §2 of the Voting Rights Act of 1965, as amended. (The Court decided that they did, with a strong dissent from Justices Scalia and Kennedy and Chief Justice Rehnquist.) As Charles Breitel, former Chief Judge of the New York Court of Appeals, wrote, "The words men use are never absolutely certain in meaning; the limitations of finite man and the even greater limitations of his language see to that." Bankers Ass'n v. Albright, 343 N.E.2d 735, 738 (N.Y. 1975).

Third, legislatures sometimes use general language, contemplating that it will be defined by administrative agencies. The constitutional propriety of such provisions is the province of administrative law. This is the topic characterized as the *delegation doctrine*. But within an appropriate delegation much is often left to administrative discretion through the use of general or nonspecific language. In one such case of statutory ambiguity, the Supreme Court determined that the judicial role is to defer to the agency's interpretation of its guiding statute. Chevron v. Natural Resources Defense Council, 467 U.S. 837 (1984).

Fourth, sometimes statutes are unclear because legislative compromises are struck to secure votes for enactment. Compromises can be struck by an agreement to leave undefined a general word or phrase in order to protect a particular political position and allow the bill to be enacted into law. Compromises also can be struck by an agreement to remain silent on a

particular point, as illustrated in Landgraf v. USI Film Products, 511 U.S. 24 (1994). In *Landgraf* the question was the effective date of certain provisions of the Civil Rights Act of 1991.
Were the provisions intended to apply to covered discriminatory acts prior to its enactment or only to such acts post its enactment? The statute did not provide an answer. The record
before the Court basically demonstrated that Congress had
agreed to disagree in order to break an impasse that had occurred on that very point. Consider the following remarks
drawn from legislative sources.

> Senator DANFORTH: My review of Supreme Court case
> law supports my reading that in the absence of an explicit pro-
> vision to the contrary, no new legislation is applied
> retroactively. Rather, new statutes are to be given prospective
> application only, unless Congress explicitly directs otherwise,
> which we have not done in this instance. 137 Cong. Rec. S15472
> (daily ed. Oct. 30, 1991).

> Senator KENNEDY: I would . . . like to state . . . my un-
> derstanding with regard to the bill's effective date. It will be up
> to the courts to determine the extent to which the bill will apply
> to cases and claims that are pending on the date of enactment.
> Ordinarily, courts in such cases apply newly enacted proce-
> dures and remedies to pending cases. . . . And where a new rule
> is merely a restoration of a prior rule that has been changed by
> the courts, the newly restored rule is often applied retroactively.
> 137 Cong. Rec. S15485 (daily ed. Oct. 30, 1991).

> Senate Staff Member: You have to decide if there are
> votes there to support this type of enactment, and we didn't
> have the votes on the left. . . . The deal was cut to make the (lan-
> guage of the) statute fairly clear and then leave it to the courts
> to pound out the issue.

Dispute over Retroactivity of Civil Rights Act Stems from Legislative History, Hill Staffer Says, 14 DLR A-13 (1992). Note the
staff member's observation. The compromise allowed the bill
to become law. For the proponents of retroactivity, the compromise meant that retroactivity was an uncertainty but that
prospective coverage was assured. For the opponents of retroactivity, the compromise meant that retroactivity remained a
possibility. From a legislative perspective this was an ideal
compromise as it did not cost support from avid proponents of

the legislation and provided the necessary additional support from legislators who favored the bill, but disfavored retroactivity. Of course, there are other perspectives. Consider, for example, the costs to litigants and the courts of testing whether provisions of the statute were retroactive or prospective. (The Court ultimately decided that the particular provisions at issue were prospective. For a discussion of a statute's effective date, see Chapter Four, section C10.)

Finally, sometimes ambiguities are created because the legislature has given insufficient thought to the meaning of the language employed or because it simply has not considered the question that has become the subject of litigation. An example of the former is the ambiguity in the applicability of the term "knowingly" in *Liparota*. A probable and interesting example of the latter is the absence of any reference to "burden of proof or persuasion" in Title VII of the Civil Rights Act of 1965. This silence resulted in two contrary decisions of the Supreme Court, Griggs v. Duke Power Co., 401 U.S. 424 (1971) (holding, among other things, that Congress placed the burden of persuasion to establish a business justification on the employer), and Wards Cove Packing Co. v. Antonio, 490 U.S. 642 (1989) (holding, among other things, that the statute required the employee to disprove a business justification raised by the employer). The issue was finally resolved in the Civil Rights Act of 1991, in which Congress, among other things, placed the burden of proving business justifications on the employer.

When the language of a statute is unclear, courts are confronted with the problem of giving meaning to a provision of a statute without clear direction from its language. In essence, they are asked to make policy choices. As courts are not simply free to "enact" their policy views into law (although recall Justice Blackmun's comments in *Weber*, page 16), they have relied on (1) general presumptions about legislative intent, known as *canons of construction*; and (2) specific presumptions about legislative intent, usually discerned through legislative history but sometimes gleaned through examining other provisions of a particular statute or the statute as a whole. As noted earlier, these tools of construction are the same ones used to establish legislative intent or purpose outside of the language of a statute. For example, the *Liparota* Court, in searching for the meaning of the ambiguous statute, finds that "[T]he legislative history of the statute contains nothing that would clarify the congressional purpose on this point," but bases its decision to require mens rea in this case on several interpretative canons, including the often cited one that "ambiguity concerning the ambit of criminal statutes should be resolved in favor of lenity." Liparota v. United States, 471 U.S. 424, 425, 427 (1985).

Note the use of the term *presumption* in the paragraph above. Legislative bodies speak through statutes, and the use of any source but the statute itself to determine its meaning is problematic. Canons of construction pose a particularly difficult case because they are judicial visions of what legislatures, in general, mean when they enact a statute. Legislative history avoids this problem because it addresses the particular procedural history of the statute in question, but it is troublesome for a different reason. Although it is grounded in the legislative process and particular to the statute in question, it is not the product of the entire legislature. Rather, it is the work of some lesser number of members, such as a committee.

3.   Two Tools for Statutory Interpretation: Canons of Construction and Legislative History

We noted above the courts' judicial use of canons of construction and legislative history as devices for statutory construction. Considerable debate has focused on this judicial use of canons and legislative history as tools for statutory interpretation. Its focus, like the focus on almost all writing about statutory interpretation, is the relationship between legislatures and courts and the powers of each institution. Below we briefly explore the issues raised in this debate to provide some context for approaching the judicial use of these devices.

a.   Canons of Construction

Canons of construction are judicially crafted maxims for determining the meaning of statutes. An example, referred to above in *Liparota*, is "ambiguity concerning the ambit of criminal statutes should be resolved in favor of lenity." Canons expressly intend to limit judicial discretion by rooting interpretive decisions in a system of aged and shared principles from which a judge may draw a "'correct,' unchallengeable rule of 'how to read.'" Karl N. Llewellyn, Remarks on the Theory of Appellate Decision and the Rules or Canons About How Statutes Are to Be Construed, 3 Vand. L. Rev. 395, 399 (1950).

There are a multitude of canons. Some of those most frequently used by the courts are listed below with their commonly used Latin phrases in parentheses. We do not, as some others do, define the plain meaning rule as a canon of construction. This is based on our view that the plain meaning rule is the constitutionally compelled starting place for any statutory construction and that tools of interpretation are only applicable when the plain meaning rule fails to provide the answer.

- A thing may be within the letter of the statute and yet not within the statute, because not within its spirit, nor within the intention of its makers.
- Statutes in derogation of the common law are to be read narrowly.
- Remedial statutes are to be read broadly.
- Criminal statutes are to be read narrowly.
- Statutes should be read to avoid constitutional questions.
- Statutes that relate to the same subject matter (*in pari materia*) are to be construed together.
- The general language of a statute is limited by specific phrases that have preceded the general language (*ejusdem generis*).
- Explicit exceptions are deemed exclusive (*expressio unius est exclusio alterius*).
- Repeals by implication are not favored.
- Words and phrases that have received judicial construction before enactment are to be understood according to that construction.
- A statute should be construed such that none of its terms are redundant.
- A statute should be read to avoid internal inconsistencies.

- Words are to be given their common meaning, unless they are technical terms or words of art.
- Titles do not control meaning.

The use of canons of construction for the interpretation of statutes has been held in scholarly ill-repute for over a century. So consistently unfavorably has their use been viewed that two contemporary scholars of statutory interpretation have matter-of-factly written that "almost everybody thinks that canons are bunk." William N. Eskridge, Jr. and Phillip P. Frickey, Cases and Materials on Legislation 630 (1988).

Two basic observations underlie this criticism of the use of canons: first, that canons are not a coherent, shared body of law from which correct answers can be drawn, and, second, that, viewed individually, many canons are wrong.

It has become commonplace to recognize that the canons are not a system or body of principles that provide the "correct reading," but are a grab bag of individual rules, from which a judge can choose to support his or her view of the case. This was Karl Llewellyn's point when he observed, in his now famous article, that "there are two opposing canons on almost every point." Karl N. Llewellyn, Remarks on the Theory of Appellate Decision and the Rules or Canons About How Statutes Are to Be Construed, 3 Vand. L. Rev. 395, 401 (1950). Few have taken issue with Llewellyn's observation. Indeed, it has been almost universally adopted as the starting place for all criticism of canons. "The usual criticism of the canons . . . is that for every canon one might bring to bear on a point there is an equal and opposite canon, so that the outcome of the inter-pretive process depends on the choice between paired oppo-sites — a choice the canons themselves do not illuminate. (You need a canon for choosing between competing canons, and there isn't any.)" Richard A. Posner, Statutory Interpretation — In the Classroom and in the Courtroom, 50 U. Chi. L. Rev. 800, 806 (1983).

Several of Llewellyn's examples illustrate the point:

- "[a] statute cannot go beyond its text" except "[t]o ef-fect its purpose a statute may be implemented beyond its text";

- "[s]tatutes in derogation of the common law will not be extended by construction," except "[s]uch acts will be liberally construed if their nature is remedial";
- "statutes *in pari materia* must be construed together," except "[a] statute is not *in pari materia* . . . where a legislative design to depart from the general purpose or policy of previous enactments may be apparent";
- "[e]very word and clause must be given effect," except "[i]f inadvertently inserted or if repugnant to the rest of the statute they may be rejected as surplusage."

Karl N. Llewellyn, Remarks on the Theory of Appellate Decision and the Rules or Canons About How Statutes Are to Be Construed, 3 Vand. L. Rev. 395, 401-406 (1950).

Canons, as individual rules, are considered equally flawed. Canons are considered presumptions about legislative intent. To see this clearly, reread the canons listed on pages 24 and 25, adding the word *why* to each. For example, Why should remedial statutes be read broadly? The answer to this question must be that this is what the enacting legislature intended, unless there is constitutional authority for another answer. But how do we know as a general proposition that when a legislature passes a remedial statute that it intends for it to be broadly applied? It is just as probable that the enacting legislature intends the statute to be moderately or narrowly applied. The point is that, as a rule, the canon bars the inquiry and is at odds with legislative supremacy (and the supremacy of legislative values of weighing, sifting, and balancing interests) by forcing the burden on the legislature to overcome a judicial presumption, rather than requiring the court to dig for the meaning. Also, assuming that a legislative body could or would undertake this burden, how would it know which canon to follow given the menu of contradictory canons?

As presumptions about the legislative process, a number of the canons are also more wrong than right and reflect little, if any, knowledge about the legislative process. Take, for example, the canon that remedial legislation should be construed broadly. Since the building of majorities necessarily requires compromise, a broad reading of a controversial statute is far more likely to undermine legislative intent than to support it. Moreover, a bill drafter's awareness of this rule of interpretation would not influence the legislative process except to guarantee the defeat of the bill if he or she were to take the position that no compromise is possible because the courts will ignore it. If a canon of interpretation is necessary, perhaps a more accurate one would be "all statutes should be construed moderately."

This tide of scholarly criticism has not eroded the judicial employment of canons as tools of interpretation. Canons, despite the criticisms, continue to provide judges (and consequently attorneys) with a necessary rationale for making interpretive choices. This is particularly true on the state level, where legislative history is slim and often inaccessible. In this context some canons make sense. For example, without legislative history to the contrary, the canon that "explicit exceptions are deemed exclusive" would seem to be useful. For an interesting discussion of the continued use of canons by the courts, see Jonathan R. Macey and Geoffrey P. Miller, The Canons of Statutory Construction and Judicial Preferences, 45 Vand. L. Rev. 647, 667 (1992) (the continued use of canons reflects an "era of moral and intellectual uncertainty"), and Lawrence C. Marshall, The Canons of Statutory Construction and Judicial Constraints: A Response to Macey and Miller, 45 Vand. L. Rev. 673 (1992) (the use of canons helps fulfill judicial obligation to legislative supremacy).

b.   Legislative History

The formal steps of the legislative process are officially documented. In Congress, ideas for legislation are introduced as bills or as amendments to bills; committee hearings, debates, and markups (committee meetings at which bills are read line by line for review and amendment) are transcribed; committee actions are set forth and explained in committee reports; legislative debate is transcribed; and votes are recorded. For all legislatures, the documentation of these steps is part of the process of building majorities and providing the public with access to the work of the legislature. For the courts, this documentation is *legislative history*. Significant steps in the legislative process are not recorded. The discussion of a bill in a political party caucus, or in the offices of a legislative leader, for example, might reveal very probative evidence of legislative intent, if documented, but, for various political reasons, it is not documented.

A legislative history of a statute might contain all or some of the following documents or documentation. (The parenthetical references are to sections of the book in which the particular step of the enactment process is discussed.)

Introduction (Chapter Three, sections C1, C2): the bill or bills through which the statute was introduced; the transcript of introductory remarks; memoranda that accompanies such introduction (New York, for example, requires introductory memoranda); and the record of a bill's assignment to committee

Committee proceedings (Chapter Two, section C3): transcripts of committee hearings, debates, and markup sessions; amendments; committee votes; and, finally, committee reports, which in Congress contain a statement of a bill's purpose and scope, a statement of the reasons for which a bill should be enacted, a section by section analysis, a statement of changes the bill would make in existing law, committee amendments to the bill, votes taken in committee, a minority report setting forth reasons for opposition to the bill

Floor proceedings (Chapter Three, sections C5-C11): transcripts of debates; floor amendments; and votes

Conference committee proceedings (Chapter Three, section C12): conference committee reports

Executive proceedings (Chapter Three, section C13): signing or veto statements and memoranda submitted in favor or opposition to the bill

Not every statute has as complete a legislative history as set forth above. Not every statute goes through every possible step of the legislative process. For example, not every statute has a hearing or is debated. Not every state legislature transcribes committee debates or includes conference committees as part of the legislative process. In beginning a search for legislative history, two initial inquiries are important: First, what legislative steps has the statute been through, and second, which of these steps are documented?

Judges use legislative history as a tool for statutory interpretation. As Justice Breyer has written, "Using legislative history to help interpret unclear statutory language seems natural. Legislative history helps a court understand the context and purpose of a statute." Stephen Breyer, On the Uses of Legislative History in Interpreting Statutes, 65 S. Cal. L. Rev. 845, 848 (1992). It seems natural because, if the judicial goal is to discover whether the legislature intended to cover the particular conduct under litigation, reference to relevant legislative history logically advances that goal. For example, recall the Court's comment in *Liparota*, page 23, about the absence of legislative history to inform the decision. Assume that there had been a committee report or a debate on the legislative floor from which it could be clearly gleaned that the intent of the legislature was to make knowledge of the conduct, alone, a crime. An example of such a case is drawn from Steadman v. Securities and Exchange Commission, 450 U.S. 91 (1981), a case referred to in many administrative law casebooks. In that case, the question before the Court was the standard of proof to be used in determining whether Steadman had violated the securities laws. In its application of §7 of the Administrative Procedure Act, the Court wrote:

[T]he language of the statute is somewhat opaque concerning the precise standard of proof to be used. The legislative history, however, clearly reveals the Congress' intent. . . . Any doubt as to the intent of Congress is removed by the House Report, which expressly adopted a preponderance-of-the-evidence standard: " . . . Where there is evidence pro and con, the agency must weigh it and decide in accordance with the preponderance. . . . "

Id. at 100-101.

The value of legislative history as a tool of statutory construction is not universally accepted. Much of the criticism has been stoked by an apparent overuse of legislative history in the last several decades. Such use of legislative history is chronicled by Judge Patricia Wald.

Two preliminary observations may be made. First, although the Court still refers to the "plain meaning" rule, the rule has effectively been laid to rest. No occasion for statutory construction now exists when the Court will *not* look at the legislative history. When the plain meaning rhetoric is invoked, it becomes a device not for ignoring legislative history but for shifting onto legislative history the burden of proving that the words do mean what they appear to say. Second, the Court has greatly expanded the types of materials and events that it will recognize in the search for congressional intent.

Patricia M. Wald, Some Observations on the Use of Legislative History in the 1981 Supreme Court Term, 68 Iowa L. Rev. 195 (1982) (emphasis added).

The criticism of the use of legislative history for statutory construction is two-pronged. First, it is argued that the use of it is inconsistent with the democratic theory encapsuled in the Constitution. "Committee reports, floor speeches, and even colloquies between Congressmen . . . are frail substitutes for bicameral vote upon the text of a law and its presentment to the President." Thompson v. Thompson, 484 U.S. 174, 191-192 (1988) (Scalia, J., concurring). In this same vein, it is said that if the goal is to find the intent of the legislature, "[l]egislative materials . . . at best can shed light only on the 'intent' of that small portion of Congress in which such records originate; [the legislative materials] therefore lack the holistic 'intent' found in the statute itself." Kenneth W. Starr, Observations about the Use of Legislative History, 1987 Duke L.J. 371, 375.

Second, serious questions have been raised about the reliability of legislative history. The sharpest example of this criticism comes from Justice Scalia.

That the Court should refer to the citation of three District Court cases in a document issued by a single committee of a single house as the action *of Congress* displays the level of unreality that our unrestrained use of legislative history has attained. . . . As anyone who is familiar with modern-day drafting of a congressional committee report is well aware, the references to the cases were inserted, at best by a committee staff member on his or her own initiative, and at worst by a committee staff member at the suggestion of a lawyer-lobbyist; and the purpose of those references was not primarily to inform the Members of Congress what the bill meant . . . but rather to influence judicial construction. What a heady feeling it must be for a young staffer, to know that his or her citation of obscure district court cases can transform them into law of the land, thereafter dutifully to be observed by the Supreme Court itself.

Blanchard v. Bergeron, 489 U.S. 87, 98-99 (1989) (Scalia J., concurring). While, in the view of the authors, Justice Scalia's general skepticism about the creation of legislative history far
overstates the problem, some corruption of the legislative record does take place. This corruption is described, in legislative
terms, as the "planting of legislative history." This refers to
adding language to the legislative record (for example, committee reports, the Congressional Record) that is not intended
to influence the legislative enactment process, but rather to influence the judicial interpretive process. As one of the authors
has previously written about his experience in Congress:

> Two members will rise and engage in a colloquy for the purpose
> of making "legislative history." Frequently, however, the collo-
> quy is written by just one of the members, not both. It is handed
> to the other actor and the two of them read it like a grade B
> radio script. And that is the material that judges later will
> solemnly pore over, under the guise of "studying the legislative
> history." This, of course, is ridiculous.

Abner J. Mikva, A Reply to Judge Starr's Observations, 1987
Duke L.J. 380, 384.

The more the courts rely on legislative history, the greater
the incentive for such corruption of the legislative record. Judicial ignorance of the legislative process also adds to the
problem because, without knowledge of the process, courts are
unable to properly assess the relative value of different pieces
of legislative history.

Consider the remarks of Senator Danforth with respect to
the enactment of the Civil Rights Act of 1991.

Mr. DANFORTH: Mr. President. I would like to say a word
this morning on the difficult, contentious subject of legislative history, what its limitations are, and how the issue of legislative history
is one that is now before the Senate.

Justice Scalia has taken the position that the Supreme Court
should not get into the business of interpreting legislative history but
that instead the Court should attempt to construe legislative
language as it appears in statutes themselves.

I think that the odyssey of the present legislation is a strong argument for Justice Scalia's position. One of the interesting things
about this particular bill is that where as with much controversial
legislation when a compromise is reached, all kinds of people say we

really do not like this bill but we are not going to be able to do any better, therefore, we will support it.

This bill is different in that a whole variety of people have come forward and have expressed support and even enthusiasm for the bill. People as diverse as the administration, on one hand, Senator DOLE, Senator HATCH and, on the other hand, for example, Senator KENNEDY, Senator MITCHELL all have expressed support. They have all said there is a lot to be said for this legislation.

One of the reasons that this is possible is that there are slightly different interpretations among Members of the Senate and between the Senate and the administration on the precise meaning of some of the provisions in the law. That is not unusual. What courts are for are to interpret what is meant by the Congress in passing laws.

It is very common for Members of the Senate to try to affect the way in which a court will interpret a statute by putting things into the Congressional Record. Sometimes statements are made on the floor of the Senate. Sometimes the Senator will say, but for such and such a provision, which I interpret in such and such a way, I never would support this bill. That is one method of trying to doctor the legislative history and influence the future course of litigation.

Another way to do it is to put interpretive memoranda in the Congressional Record. These memoranda typically are not read on the floor of the Senate. They are just stuck into the [Congressional] Record.

Another way to do it is for agreed colloquies to be signed by various Senators and for those to be stuck into the [Congressional] Record. This is what is happening with respect to this bill. Last Friday, Senator KENNEDY made a speech on the floor of the Senate. He stated his views of what the bill does. Senator HATCH has just made a very extensive speech on the floor. He stated his views of what the bill does.

My guess, Mr. President, is that if Senator KENNEDY would give us his analysis of Senator HATCH's position he would disagree with it. If Senator HATCH would give us his analysis of Senator KENNEDY's position, Senator HATCH would disagree with Senator KENNEDY. I might disagree with both of them. I anticipate that I am going to have an interpretive memorandum which will be put into the [Congressional] Record signed by the other original six Republican cosponsors for the legislation. That will be our interpretation of various provisions, but it may not be the interpretation of Senator HATCH or Senator KENNEDY or anybody else.

So what I am saying is that Justice Scalia, I think, has a good point in stating that it is risky business to try to piece together from floor statements or from agreed memoranda legislative history which is informative to the court in interpreting the meaning of a statute. . . .

I believe, Mr. President, we should go ahead and pass the bill. I believe that it will be passed. But I simply want to state that a court would be well advised to take with a large grain of salt floor debate and statements placed into the Congressional Record which purport to create an interpretation for the legislation that is before us.

Cong. Rec. S15,324-15,325 (daily ed. Oct. 29, 1991). The passages emphasized in the above-quoted passage from the debate over the Civil Rights Act of 1991 demonstrate why the language of a statute is sometimes unclear. The need to pass a statute brings with it the need to compromise. Sometimes such compromises are in the form of obscuring the particular meaning of a statute, allowing different legislators to read the obscured provisions the way they wish.

A third criticism of the use of legislative history comes from a legislative perspective. This criticism was well stated by M. Douglass Bellis, Assistant Legislative Counsel, U.S. House of Representatives, at the 1996 American Association of Law Professors' annual conference: "If we decide that the legislative history . . . is more important than the legislation, legislators will never really know what they have to do, what levers they need to pull in order to get their ideas firmly cemented in place."

The debate over the use of legislative history has another focus beyond the reliability of particular pieces of such history and its democratic legitimacy. As we noted earlier, approaches to statutory interpretation also reflect choices concerning the exercise of political power. From this perspective, the failure to use appropriate legislative history as a basis for resolving a dispute over the meaning of an ambiguous statute can be seen as opting for judicial dominance of the interpretive arena. If legislative history is ignored, what is effectively left as a basis for decision are canons of construction, which, as discussed in section B3a of this chapter, effectively permit unfettered discretion.

What seems in order is not the avoidance of legislative history, but its careful use. Legislative history is, after all, part of the legislative process, and the outright refusal to acknowledge it as a vehicle for expressing legislative intent raises constitutional questions. Consider the following view of Judge Wald:

> If we are serious about respecting the will of Congress, how can we ignore Congress' chosen methods for expressing that will? For all its imperfections, legislative history, in the form of committee reports, hearings, and floor remarks, is available to courts because Congress has made those documents available to us. . . . As Justice Scalia has recognized, there does indeed exist a congressional practice of including information in legislative history for the purpose, among others, of informing later judicial construction of the statute. But, to the extent that Congress performs its responsibilities through committees and delegates to staff the writing of its reports, it is Congress' evident intention that an explanation of what it has done be obtained from these extrinsic materials. If only a few of the "sneakier" members of Congress were slipping information past the congressional membership at large, I might share Justice Scalia's skepticism of giving any weight to legislative history. That, however, is not the case; legislative history is the authoritative product of the institutional work of the Congress. It records the manner in which Congress enacts its legislation, and it represents the way Congress communicates with the country at large.
>
> To disregard committee reports as indicators of congressional understanding because we are suspicious that nefarious staffers have planted certain information for some undisclosed reason, is to second-guess Congress' chosen form of organization and delegation of authority, and to doubt its ability to oversee its own constitutional functions effectively. It comes perilously close, in my view, to impugning the way a coordinate branch conducts its operations and, in that sense, runs the risk of violating the spirit if not the letter of the separation of powers principle.

Patricia M. Wald, The Sizzling Sleeper: The Use of Legislative History in Construing Statutes in the 1988-89 Term of the United States Supreme Court, 39 Am. U. L. Rev. 277, 306-307 (1990).

Careful use would prevent the use of legislative history to contradict clear language, unless its application was clearly absurd. Too frequently, a court refers to legislative history, notwithstanding its own recognition of the clarity of the language. It is the language of the statute that is the "constitutional center of focal awareness." Reed Dickerson, The Interpretation and Application of Statutes 144 (1975). Legislatures vote on bill language. No bill becomes law unless identical text is agreed on by a majority of each house of the legislature. The president must have an opportunity to approve or veto this language; if vetoed, the legislature is given the opportunity to override the veto of that language; and it is the statute that informs the public of the regulation. Allowing legislative history to trump clear legislative language also, as Mr. Bellis noted, creates legislative uncertainly as to how to fix policy into law. For a unique case in which the Supreme Court uses legislative history to trump clear statutory language, see Train v. Colorado Public Interest Research Group, Inc., 426 U.S. 1 (1976). In this case the Court of Appeals had written:

> In our view, then, the statute is plain and unambiguous and should be given its obvious meaning. Such being the case, . . . we need not here concern ourselves with the legislative history of the 1972 amendments.

Colorado Public Interest Group, Inc. v. Train, 507 F.2d 743, 748 (10th Cir. 1974). To which the Supreme Court, in reversing the Court of Appeals, replied:

> To the extent that the Court of Appeals excluded reference to the legislative history of the [statute] in discerning its meaning, the court was in error. As we have noted before: "When aid to construction of the meaning of words, as used in the statute, is available, there certainly can be no 'rule of law' which forbids its use, however clear the words may appear on 'superficial examination.'"

Train v. Colorado Public Interest Group, Inc., 426 U.S. 1, 10 (1976). Of course, on other occasions the Court has also stated the more traditional prescription: "When confronted with a statute which is plain and unambiguous on its face, we ordinarily do not look to legislative history as a guide to its meaning." Tennessee Valley Authority v. Hill, 437 U.S. 153, 185 n.29 (1978). The Supreme Court of Oregon formalized this view in its admonition that "if, but only if, the intent of the legislature is not clear from the text and context inquiry, the court will then move to the second level, which is to consider the legislative history." Portland General Electric Co. v. Bureau of Labor and Industries, 859 P.2d 1143, 1146 (Or. 1993).

Careful use would also entail a judicial understanding of the legislative process and a good-faith attempt on the part of the courts to choose legislative history that is most probative of legislative intent and not legislative history that supports their views. For, as Justice Jackson stated, "It is a poor cause that cannot find some plausible support in legislative history." Robert H. Jackson, Problems of Statutory Interpretation, 8 F.R.D. 121, 125 (1948).

For a piece of legislative history to be probative of legislative intent, it must bear a significant relationship to the enactment process. Within this broad category, legislative history can then be prioritized by levels of significance. For Congress, the following rough pecking order for choosing legislative history makes sense:

1. Committee reports (including conference reports),
2. Markup transcripts (described on page 91),
3. Committee debate and hearing transcripts,
4. Transcripts of "hot" (actual) floor debate.

The significance of committee reports needs reemphasis. Congress acts through committees (see Chapter Two, section C3), and "in the ordinary course of legislation, committee reports should be looked to for the most coherent, thorough, and authoritative explanation of a bill's purpose and intended meaning." George A. Costello, Average Voting Members and Other "Benign Fictions": The Relative Reliability of Committee Reports, Floor Debates, and Other Sources of Legislative History, 1990 Duke L.J. 39, 72. As Professor Correia has written, "Legislators . . . are wary of freewheeling uses of legislative history. We should assume that legislators want courts to consider primarily statements that are adopted by the majority or that represent explanations by legislators with specialized responsibility for enactment." Edward O. Correia, A Legislative Conception of Legislative Supremacy, 42 Case W. Res. L. Rev. 1129, 1157 (1992).

Statements made on the floor, which are not part of an actual debate, or statements inserted in the Congressional Record (see Chapter Three, section B) should mostly be ignored. So, too, should statements by the opponents of legislation, except in the hot debate context. Consider the following experience of Judge Mikva during his tenure in Congress.

When the provisions of the Organized Crime Act of 1970 [RICO] came up for floor debate, I expressed my opposition in hyperbolic terms, parading one horrible example after another before the House. Since the managers had the number of votes needed for passage, and I was speaking mostly to an empty House, they did not even bother to answer me. My remarks have been used ever since as legislative history to prove the broad scope of RICO.

Abner J. Mikva, Reading and Writing Statutes, 48 U. Pitt. L. Rev. 627, 632 (1987). Statements made on the floor as part of the debate must be weighed according to their significance to the debate. For example, Professor Ross suggests two categories of statements that he (and we concur) considers most reliable:

(1) statements by the sponsor of the legislation or the particular provision at issue when it appears that members who might otherwise desire to amend the bill have relied on those statements; and (2) colloquies between the "major players" concerning a legislative provision when it appears that the majority of members are prepared to follow any consensus reached by these individuals.

Stephen F. Ross, Where Have You Gone, Karl Llewellyn? Should Congress Turn Its Lonely Eyes to You?, 45 Vand. L. Rev. 561, 576 (1992).

On occasion, courts refer to the rejection of amendments during the enactment process as evidence of one of the meanings being urged in a litigation. This is a dangerous exercise, for "[t]here are many reasons for saying no." Reed Dickerson, The Interpretation and Application of Statutes 160 (1975). For example, the rejection of an amendment could reflect the view that the amendment is superfluous.

Another problematic interpretive exercise is the use of legislative silence to confirm prior judicial statutory constructions. "It is at best treacherous to find in legislative silence alone the adoption of a controlling rule of law." Girouard v. United States, 328 U.S. 61, 69 (1946). The typical case unfolds as follows: Confronted with an unclear statute, a court finds an earlier decision that interprets the language in a particular way. The court then justifies its use of this earlier interpretation by stating that the earlier interpretation has been

legislatively adopted because the legislature has failed to overturn it. Assuming that legislators are generally aware of
judicial decisions (which, in most instances, is a false assumption), there are numerous reasons why a legislature might not
overturn the decision. Professors Hart and Sacks, in their
landmark book, offer many:

> Complete disinterest; Belief that other measures have a stronger
> claim on the limited time and energy of the body; Belief that the
> bill is sound in principle but politically inexpedient to be con-
> nected with; Unwillingness to have the bill's sponsors get credit
> for its enactment; Belief that the bill is sound in principle but de-
> fective in material particulars; Tentative approval, but belief
> that action should be withheld until the problem can be
> attacked on a broader front; Indecision, with or without one or
> another of the foregoing attitudes also; Belief that the matter
> should be left to be handled by the normal processes of judicial
> development of decisional law, including the overruling of
> outstanding decisions to the extent that the sound growth of the
> law requires; Positive approval of existing law as expressed in
> outstanding decisions of the Supreme Court; Ditto of the courts
> of appeals' decisions also; Ditto also of district court decisions;
> Ditto also of one or more varieties of outstanding administra-
> tive determinations; Etc., etc., etc., etc., etc.

Henry M. Hart, Jr. and Albert M. Sacks, The Legal Process: Basic Problems in the Making and Application of Law 1395-1396
(1958).

A variation on the "use" of legislative silence is found in
Girouard. At issue was whether Girouard's stated unwilling-
ness to take up arms on behalf of the United States (he was
willing to serve in the armed forces) disqualified him for citizenship. The question was the meaning of the statutorily prescribed oath of allegiance for becoming a citizen. Neither the
oath nor other provisions of the statute answered the question,
but, prior to 1942, several Supreme Court decisions had interpreted the language of the oath as requiring an applicant to be
willing to take up arms in defense of the country. Many attempts to reverse these decisions had died in legislative
committees.

Standing alone, these efforts should have no impact on the
statute's interpretation for the reasons discussed earlier. What
makes this case particularly interesting is that in 1942 Con-

gress reenacted the oath without change, raising the question for the court of whether this reenactment without change incorporated the interpretation of the oath stated in the Court's several earlier decisions. In other words, the question after the reenactment became whether Congress had adopted the Court's earlier view that the oath of allegiance included implicitly an obligation to bear arms for the United States. The Court, as noted by the earlier quoted passage, refused to infuse legislative silence with such meaning, but it was clear from the decision that the Court thought its earlier decisions incorrect. Despite our wariness over the use of legislative silence, and without consideration of the policies in dispute in *Girouard*, it would seem that such a procedural record could reasonably be read to support the view that in 1942 Congress had adopted the interpretation of the oath declared by the earlier Court decisions. This is the rule that most courts apply.

Postenactment explanations of legislative meaning would seem absolutely taboo. For example, a postenactment letter from a senator to an administrative agency head informing that head what the senator believed a piece of legislation meant, because that senator was involved in its enactment, should have no probative value. First, such postenactment statements are not part of the enactment process. Second, they are absolutely unreliable. All postenactment statements by legislators are influenced by postenactment political considerations. An experience of one of the authors, Professor Lane, illustrates this point. The New York State legislature wanted to block an attempt by a county legislature to take over a nuclear power plant. To accomplish its purpose, the state legislature enacted preemptive legislation. In a subsequent litigation over whether the state statute preempted the local law, several members of the state legislature, who had voted in favor of the state legislation, attempted to submit affidavits declaring that the legislation was not intended to be preemptive. All of these members had participated in negotiating the bill and were well aware of its purpose. But subsequent to the adoption of the state legislation, they had become the target of intense protests by local legislators and community groups, who claimed that the state legislation denied them home rule and inadequately protected local interests. The affidavits were reflective of these later pressures, rather than of the legislative history.

In recent years, some commentators have argued for judicial use of executive signing statements in statutory interpretation. The argument in favor of this position rests on the role of the executive in the legislative process. (See Chapter Two, section A3.) The signing message is not a part of the enactment process. While the President has the power to veto a bill and the legislature has the power to override the veto, the legislature has no power to veto or override the executive's signing message, which can contain any statement the executive chooses to include. For example, at issue in Chisom v. Roemer, 501 U.S. 380 (1991) was whether the word *representative* in §2 of the Voting Rights Act of 1965, as amended by the Voting Rights Amendments of 1982, included elected judges. (See Chapter Four for excerpts of both acts.) The majority decided that it did. Assume, that in signing the Voting Rights Amendments of 1982, President Reagan had specifically stated that he was signing the bill based on his understanding that the term *representative* did not include elected judges. In our view, this signing statement should not be used in interpreting the statute because it has not been the subject of legislative consideration but is simply executive gloss about which the legislature can do nothing. By this we mean that Congress cannot debate or override, as part of the enactment process, a signing statement accompanying an approved bill. We would make one exception to this view. Assume that in the signing statement the executive made reference to some communication or negotiation between the executive and the legislative leadership in which agreement had been reached over the meaning declared in the signing statement. In such a case, a signing statement might have some probative value. Despite our view on signing statements, they should not be ignored in the practice of law, particularly on the state level. State courts often make reference to them, probably because of the absence of legislatively generated materials and the need of courts to hang their decisions on some peg of the enactment process. For a detailed discussion of executive signing statements, see William D. Popkin, Judicial Use of Presidential Legislative History: A Critique, 66 Ind. L.J. 699 (1991).

From the above discussion, a cautionary lesson should be evident. Generalizations about the probative value of legislative history are only useful as general guidelines for statutory interpretation. Knowing, for example, that the committee reports are an extremely important part of congressional practice alerts one to the importance of committee reports but does not answer the question of whether a particular committee report is important for determining legislative intent with respect to a particular provision of a statute. Every statute has its own legislative history that must be explored in the search for the meaning of the particular statutory language.

State legislatures offer little comparable opportunities to follow their activities. While all state legislatures record or transcribe their sessions, the accessibility of these records varies from state to state. Less available are the transcripts of committee meetings and hearings. Some state legislatures produce committee reports; others do not. For example, New York does not, but it does require a sponsor's explanatory memorandum with the introduction of legislation.

4.   "Show-Down" Questions

Sometimes the meaning of an unclear statute cannot be clarified by reference to other provisions of the statute, traditional canons, or legislative history. In other words, sometimes the meaning of a statute cannot be found through an exploration of the legislative process. This is particularly true on the state level where legislative history is sparsely documented and access to those documents is not easy. "[I]n New York and likely other states as well, legislative history is relatively sparse with legislative intent evidenced primarily by the language of the statute itself." Judith S. Kaye, State Courts at the Dawn of a New Century: Common Law Courts Reading Statutes and Constitutions, 70 N.Y.U. L. Rev. 1, 30 (1995).

It is such a situation that Professor Harry W. Jones characterizes as a "'serious business' situation" or a "show-down question," one for which statutory sources or legislative procedures cannot provide an answer and yet the court must. Harry W. Jones, An Invitation to Jurisprudence, 74 Colum. L. Rev. 1023, 1041 (1974). According to Jones:

> In "serious business" situations, the positive law is not a command to the judge but, at most, an authorization of alternative

decisions. Judges, by and large, are reluctant lawmakers, but the role is thrust upon even the most modest of them by the realities of their function. The case must be decided, one way or the other. Unlike the pure social scientist, the judge cannot withhold his action until all the returns are in. There is no hiding place from the political and moral obligation to decide.

Id. at 1041. The phrase *serious business* is drawn from Justice Cardozo: "It is when the colors do not match, when the references in the index fail, when there is no decisive precedent, that the serious business of the judge begins." Benjamin N. Cardozo, The Nature of the Judicial Process 21 (1921). One point of Professor Jones's observation needs particular emphasis. Faced with a show-down question, even the most deferential judges must become "activists" in the sense that they must resolve the question before them without legislative guidance. This point is illustrated by federal District Court Judge Nicholas Politan in answer to a question concerning show-down cases: "You have litigators in front of you, you have people who want answers to their problems. What do you have to do? It seems to me in a situation where there is nothing to look to you have to search out the legislative intent in any method that you deem proper." Proceedings of the Twenty-First Annual United States Judicial Conference for the District of New Jersey (March 13, 1997).

In practice, judges do not clearly signal that a particular question of interpretation is a show-down question. Such expression offends concepts of separation of power and could lead to questions about the judge's willingness to obey his or her obligation to effect legislative purpose. Instead, judges frame these decisions along traditional lines, with strained references to legislative purpose or intent. Circuit Court Judge Robert Cowen makes this point powerfully: "I think I have to be brutally honest with you and say the unspeakable, that I would decide the case based on what I perceive to be the most just manner of resolving the matter before me, and that all of these tools of legislative history, canons and so forth, would merely be techniques that I would employ to write a decision." Proceedings of the Twenty-First Annual United States Judicial Conference for the District of New Jersey (March 13, 1997).

About this process, Professor Jones has observed:

Why is it so hard to tell, on a first reading of the court's opinion in a "serious business" case, that the controversy was originally a stand-off, as concerns formal legal doctrine, and was decided as it was chiefly in accordance with the court's views — informed judgment, intuitive impression, or largely unconscious predilection, depending on judge or judges involved — of what is sound public policy? The source of the analytical difficulty is in the syllogistic form characteristic of judicial opinions, which operates, as often as not to obscure policy decisions in a wrapping of essentially secondary doctrinal explanations. For courts must not only reach decisions, they also have to justify them, and, as John Dewey wrote a long time ago, there is always danger that the logic of justification will overpower and conceal the logic of search inquiry by which a decision was actually arrived at.

Harry W. Jones, An Invitation to Jurisprudence, 74 Colum. L. Rev. 1023, 1041 (1974). An example of a decision in which a court signals that it faces a show-down question and basically confronts it head on is Braschi v. Stahl Associates.

Braschi v. Stahl Associates, 543 N.E.2d 49 (N.Y. 1989). In *Braschi*, New York's highest court, the Court of Appeals, was required to interpret the term *family* in a rent control statute. The statute regulated the amounts of rent that could be charged for certain apartments and the landlord's right to evict tenants. Braschi had lived with another man, Leslie Blanchard, in a rent-controlled apartment. Their lives were completely socially and economically intertwined and both considered the apartment they lived in their home. Blanchard had signed the lease. Blanchard died. Under the statute, if Braschi was a member of Blanchard's family, he could not be evicted from the apartment. If he was not, he could be. The statute contained no definition of the term *family*, nor was one discernible from the statute's legislative history. Also, as the plurality of the court pointed out, the dictionary allowed for both definitions of family. According to Webster's Dictionary, *family* could be defined as: (1) "all the people living in the same house" or (2) "a group consisting of the two parents and their children." The purpose of the statute was, as the court agreed, indisputable. The act was passed both to protect a narrow group of occupants, "familial" tenants, from eviction and to gradually return rent-controlled apartments to the free market.

Based on the above, for a majority of the court the "legis-lative intent . . . [was] completely indecipherable" (Bellacosa, J., in concurrence). The court opted for the broader definition, protecting Braschi's tenancy. In its reasoning, the majority divided into a three-member plurality and a single concur-rence. At first, the plurality justified its decision by stringing together a series of selected canons, which, on careful reading, do not seem to add anything to the debate:

> It is fundamental that in construing the words of a statute "[t]he legislative intent is the great and controlling principle." Indeed, "the general purpose is a more important aid to the meaning than any rule which grammar or formal logic may lay down." Statutes are ordinarily interpreted so as to avoid objec-tionable consequences and to prevent hardship or injustice. Hence, where doubt exists as to the meaning of a term, and a choice between two constructions is afforded, the consequences that may result from the different interpretations should be con-sidered. In addition, since rent-control laws are remedial in na-ture and designed to promote the public good, their provisions should be interpreted broadly to effectuate their purposes. Fi-nally, where a problem as to the meaning of a given term arises, a court's role is not to delve into the minds of legislators, but rather to effectuate the statute by carrying out the purpose of the statute as it is embodied in the words chosen by the Legislature.

Id. at 208. But by the end of their decision, the court stated its view: "We conclude that the term family, as used in . . . [the statute], should not be rigidly restricted to those people who have formalized their relationship by obtaining, for instance, a marriage certificate or an adoption order. The intended protec-tion against sudden eviction should not rest on fictitious legal distinctions or genetic history, but instead should find its foundation in the reality of family life." Id. at 210.

Judge Bellacosa in concurrence stated the interpretative dilemma more clearly:

> [C]ourts, in circumstances as are presented here where legislative intent is completely indecipherable . . . are not em-powered or expected to expand or to constrict the meaning of the legislatively chosen word "family," which could have been and still can be qualified or defined by the duly constituted enacting body in satisfying its separate branch responsibility

and prerogative. Construing a [statute] does not allow sub-
stitution of judicial views or preferences for those of the
enacting body when the latter either fails or is unable or
deliberately refuses to specify criteria or definitional limits for
its selected umbrella word, "family," especially where the
societal, governmental, policy and fiscal implications are so
sweeping. . . . The plurality opinion favors the petitioner's side
by invoking the nomenclature of "nuclear normal"/"genuine"
family versus the "traditional"/"legally recognizable" family
selected by the dissenting opinion in favor of the landlord. I
eschew both polar camps because I see no valid reason for
deciding so broadly; indeed, there are cogent reasons not to
yaw towards either end of the spectrum.

[T]he application of the governing word and statute to
reach a decision in this case can be accomplished on a narrow
and legitimate jurisprudential track. The enacting body has selected an unqualified word for a socially remedial statute, intended as a protection against one of the harshest decrees
known to the law — eviction from one's home. Traditionally, in
such circumstances, generous construction is favored. . . . The
reasons for my position in this case are as plain as the
inappropriate criticism of the dissent that I have engaged in *ipse
dixit* decision making. It should not be that difficult to
appreciate my view that no more need be decided or said in this
case under the traditional discipline of the judicial process.
Interstitial adjudication, when a court cannot institutionally
fashion a majoritarian rule of law either because it is fragmented
or because it is not omnipotent, is quite respectable jurisprudence. We just do not know the answers or implications for
an exponential number of varied fact situations, so we should
do what courts are in the business of doing — deciding cases as
best they fallibly can. Applying the unvarnished regulatory
word, "family," as written, to the facts so far presented falls
within a well-respected and long-accepted judicial method.

Id. at 214, 215. Perhaps in partial response to Judge Bellacosa,
New York's Chief Judge Judith S. Kaye, a member of the
Braschi plurality as an associate judge, has written: "I think it
clear that common law courts interpreting statutes and filling
the gaps have no choice but to 'make law' in circumstances
where neither the statutory text not the 'legislative will' provides a single clear answer." Judith S. Kaye, State Courts at the
Dawn of a New Century: Common Law Courts Reading Statutes and Constitutions, 70 N.Y.U. L. Rev. 1, 33 (1995).

It is also difficult to determine whether a court is facing a show-down for a second reason. The judges deciding the case may simply disagree on the question. As easy as it is to define a show-down question in general, such definition can be very elusive in the context of a particular case. Judges on a panel may disagree over whether a particular case presents such a question, based on each one's perception of a statute or the importance that each places on legislative history or particular items thereof. For example, is the question of whether "a voluntary affirmative action plan that discriminates against whites prohibited by the Civil Rights Act of 1964" (presented in United Steelworkers of America, AFL-CIO-CLC v. Weber, supra at pages 14-16) a show-down question? To the Supreme Court dissenters and to many commentators, including the authors, it is not. To the Supreme Court majority, or to some of its members (certainly Justice Blackmun), it might have been.

5. *Judicial Review of Agency Interpretations*

In the age of statutes, administrative agencies have been the vehicles for implementing many of the statutory schemes. Each major regulatory effort — from efforts to regulate trusts and the air waves to the social legislation of the 1930s, civil rights legislation of the 1960s, and environmental legislation of the 1970s — has birthed a new agency or enhanced the regulatory power of an old one, for example, the Federal Trade Commission, the Federal Communications Commission, the Social Security Administration, the Equal Employment Opportunities Commission, and the Environmental Protection Agency. Central to the agency function is the interpretation of its enabling legislation, which establishes its mission. This means that, in many litigations, courts are reviewing decisions by agencies about the meaning of their enabling statutes. Agencies, like the courts, are required to defer to the plain meaning rule, and the failure of an agency to do so is reversible by a court. But in a case in which the statute is unclear, the Supreme Court has held that federal courts must defer to the interpretation given to the statute by that agency to which Congress has delegated the power to apply the statute. The Court's reasoning follows:

When a court reviews an agency's construction of the statute which it administers, it is confronted with two questions. First, always, is the question whether Congress has directly spoken to the precise question at issue. If the intent of Congress is clear, that is the end of the matter; for the court, as well as the agency, must give effect to the unambiguously expressed intent of Congress. If, however, the court determines Congress has not directly addressed the precise question at issue, the court does not simply impose its own construction on the statute, as would be necessary in the absence of an administrative interpretation. Rather, if the statute is silent or ambiguous with respect to the specific issue, the question for the court is whether the agency's answer is based on a permissible construction of the statute. . . .

If Congress has explicitly left a gap for the agency to fill, there is an express delegation of authority to the agency to elucidate a specific provision of the statute by regulation. Such legislative regulations are given controlling weight unless they are arbitrary, capricious, or manifestly contrary to the statute. Sometimes the legislative delegation to an agency on a particular question is implicit rather than explicit. In such a case, a court may not substitute its own construction of a statutory provision for a reasonable interpretation made by the administrator of an agency. . . .

Chevron v. Natural Resources Defense Council, 467 U.S. 837, 842-844 (1984).

Several observations about *Chevron* deserve note. First, as might be expected, the Court's decision has not proved easy to apply. Whether legislative intent is clear or unclear is not as easy to determine as might be initially thought, particularly if judges do not like the consequence of finding the statute clear (that is, the agency's interpretation). Second, the Court's rendering in effect creates a new canon of construction. As discussed earlier in this chapter, canons are presumptions of legislative intent. Applying this standard to *Chevron*, one needs to answer the following question: Why should courts give deference to agency interpretations of unclear statutes? As a presumption of legislative intent, this one, like many of the others discussed earlier, is sometimes correct and sometimes not correct. Congress frequently delegates policy making to administrative agencies either through broad grants of power or through general language. But not every provision of a regulatory statute is a delegation of power to an agency. As Professor Sunstein has written:

> Such a rule is quite appealing, especially when Congress has delegated law-interpreting power to the agency or when the question involves the agency's specialized fact finding and policy making competence. . . .
>   For several reasons, however, a general rule of judicial deference to all agency interpretations of law would be unsound. The case for deference depends in the first instance on congressional instructions. If Congress has told courts to defer to agency interpretations, courts must do so. But many regulatory statutes were born out of legislative distrust for agency discretion; they represent an effort to limit administrative authority through clear legislative specifications. A rule of deference in the face of ambiguity would be inconsistent with understandings, endorsed by Congress, of the considerable risks posed by administrative discretion. An ambiguity is simply not a delegation of law-interpreting power. *Chevron* confuses the two.

Cass R. Sunstein, Interpreting Statutes in the Regulatory State, 103 Harv. L. Rev. 405, 445 (1989).

Third, *Chevron* makes the president a direct player in the process of statutory interpretation. Prior to *Chevron*, the president's affirmative role (not including the veto power) was essentially one of lobbyist, and the legislative intent of the Congress that enacted the legislation would, at least in theory, control any interpretive decision. After *Chevron*, the president, through the control of administrative agencies, has a far more important role. Consider the following provision from President Bush's signing statement for the Civil Rights Act of 1991:

> This change in the burden of proof . . . means it is especially important to ensure that all the legislation's other safeguards against unfair application of disparate impact law are carefully observed. These highly technical matters are addressed in detail in the analyses of S. 1745 placed in the legislative record by Senator Dole on behalf of himself and several other Senators and of the Administration. I direct that these documents be treated as authoritative interpretive guidance by all officials in the Executive branch with respect to the law of disparate impact as well as other matters covered in the documents.

Id. Senator Dole, along with the administration, had argued for a narrow statute, a view reflected in the materials referred to in the signing statement. In the end, although the statute was not as narrow as the bill Senator Dole had advocated, he supported the enacted legislation, offering his narrow reading (the analysis referred to in the signing statement) as justification for his vote. Assume that the relevant agencies followed the command of the president set forth in his signing statement. Before *Chevron,* courts would not have credited such agency action as having interpretive value; after *Chevron* such activity would be entitled to deference if the statute was unclear. See generally Cynthia Farina, Statutory Interpretation and the Balance of Power in the Administrative State, 89 Colum. L. Rev. 452 (1989).

Fourth, by removing references to legislative intent as a tool for interpreting unclear regulatory statutes, *Chevron* reduces the power of the Congress that enacted the statute. While much of the power goes to the president and the relevant agencies, the decision also enhances the authority of the current Congress and especially its oversight committees. This is because, in the case of an ambiguous statute, the agency can no longer rely on legislative history to defend itself against legislative influence by arguing about the meaning intended by the enacting legislature, as evidenced by the statute's history. See generally Peter Strauss, When the Judge Is Not the Primary Official with Responsibility to Read: Agency Interpretation and the Problem of Legislative History, 66 Chi.-Kent L. Rev. 321, 335 (1990). As Professor Strauss has written, "part of what distinguishes agencies from courts in the business of statute-reading is that if we accept a legitimate role for current politics in the work of agencies, the question then becomes . . . how much law there is in the mixture." Id. at 335.

Of course, in enacting a statute, Congress can avoid subsequent shifts of power by drafting its statutes to avoid the *Chevron* consequence. For a very interesting book advocating that Congress exercise more control over agencies by drafting tighter statutes, see David Schoenbrod, Power without Responsibility, How Congress Abuses the People through Delegation (1993). Congress could also amend §706 of the Administrative Procedure Act to prohibit the courts from giving deference to administrative interpretations of unclear statutes.

State courts generally have not adopted the *Chevron* canon. While state courts give weight in various circumstances to agency interpretations of their enabling statutes, they tend to reserve to themselves, in some form or another, the authority to impose their interpretations of statutes that do not call for the application of an agency's particular expertise. See generally Arthur E. Bonfield and Michael Asimow, State and Federal Administrative Law (1989).

C. TRADITIONAL AND CONTEMPORARY THEORIES OF STATUTORY INTERPRETATION

In the first section of this chapter, we explored the methods courts have traditionally used to establish (or claim to establish) the meaning of statutes and provided some critiques along the way. Stated simply, statutes are commands of the legislature that must be followed by the courts. The starting point for statutory interpretation is the language of the statute. Sometimes a court will not or cannot apply the language of a statute and will look elsewhere — to other provisions of the statute or to the legislative history or to canons of interpretation — to find the statute's meaning in the context of the particular case. A clear judicial statement of this traditional approach is found in Portland General Electric Co. v. Bureau of Labor and Industries, 859 P.2d 1143 (Or. 1993), in which the Oregon Supreme Court established the following levels of interpretive analysis:

1. the text and context of the statutory provision, as a starting point;
2. the legislative history, if, but only if, the intent is not clear from the text and context legislative;
3. canons of construction, if the legislative history does not provide an answer.

Characteristic of the traditional approach is the search for legislative meaning, even in the hardest of cases. This is true even in the show-down cases in which, by definition, legislative meaning is elusive and in which judicial reference to legislative meaning is almost fictional. The overriding concern is to avoid opening the door to judicial lawmaking.

The recent decade has seen an explosion in scholarly attention to statutory interpretation. With it has come a bevy of new terms and insights into the processes by which judges interpret statutes, criticisms of the traditional approach, and numerous suggestions of how it ought to be corrected. At the heart of most of this new writing remains what Judge Posner has called, and we quote again, "the important question concerning statutory interpretation, which is political rather than epistemic: how free *should* judges feel themselves to be from the fetters of text and legislative intent in applying statutes." Richard A. Posner, The Problems of Jurisprudence 271 (1990). For example, recognizing the continued force of canons, several scholars urge the adoption of "new" canons of construction as part of their theories on how courts should interpret statutes. Professor Sunstein, for example, advocates a creative role for courts confronting unclear statutes. He argues for a series of canons "that improve the performance of modern government, and that are not based on pre-New Deal understandings, which seem to have overstayed their welcome." Cass R. Sunstein, Interpreting Statutes in the Regulatory State, 103 Harv. L. Rev. 405, 412 (1989). Under this series of canons, courts would be authorized "to promote accountability and deliberation in government, to furnish surrogates when both [accountability and deliberation] are absent, to limit factionalism and self-interested representation, and to further political equality." Id. at 477.

Judge (then Professor) Easterbrook, on the other hand, would limit the redistributive or regulatory effects of statutes through a "meta" canon that constrains the applicability of statutes "to cases anticipated by the [statutory] framers and expressly resolved in the legislative process." Frank H. Easterbrook, Statutes' Domain, 50 U. Chi. L. Rev. 533, 544 (1983).

> My suggestion is that unless the statute plainly hands courts the power to create and revise a form of common law [for example, federal antitrust legislation], the domain of the statutes should be restricted to cases anticipated by its framers and expressly resolved in the legislative process. Unless the

party relying on the statute could establish either express resolution or creation of the common law power of revision, the court would hold the matter in question outside the statute's domain. The statute would become irrelevant, the parties (and court) remitted to whatever other sources of law might be applicable. . . .

Id. Arguably, the effect of such a canon would re-create a form of nineteenth-century judicial conservatism captured by the earlier canon, "statutes in derogation of the common law should be read narrowly."

Such thinking also lies at the base of what is referred to as *New Textualism.* Under this approach to statutory interpretation, made well known by Justices Scalia and Thomas, only the text of the statutory provision at issue and the text of the body of law into which the provision has been integrated is to be used in statutory interpretation; if the text fails, canons of construction may be consulted. The key to understanding New Textualism is its abhorrence to any reference to a statute's legislative history. An example of this approach is the dissent by Justice Thomas, joined by Justice Scalia, in Holder v. Hall, 113 S. Ct. 2581 (1994), in which he argued that legislative districting plans are not subject to the Voting Rights Act of 1965 because they are not expressly mentioned in the statute, despite the fact that the legislative history of the act makes its applicability to districting plans clear and that almost all Voting Rights regulation and litigation from 1965 onward has been over districting plans. Of course, the effect of excluding the districting plans would be to narrow the Voting Rights Act to almost irrelevance.

From a contrary perspective, Professor Eskridge argues that courts should (and do) look to "current policies and societal conditions" to resolve unclear statutes.

The static vision of statutory interpretation prescribed by traditional doctrine is strikingly outdated. In practice, it imposes unrealistic burdens on judges, asking them to extract textual meaning that makes sense in the present from historical materials whose sense is often impossible to recreate faithfully. As doctrine, it is intellectually antediluvian, in light of recent developments in the philosophy of interpretation. Interpretation is not static, but dynamic. Interpretation is not an archeological discovery, but a dialectical creation. Interpretation is not mere exegesis to pinpoint historical meaning, but hermeneutics to apply that meaning to current problems and circumstances. . . .

Under dynamic statutory interpretation, the textual perspective is critical in many cases. The traditional understanding of the "rule of law" requires that statutes enacted by the majoritarian legislature be given effect, and that citizens have reasonable notice of the legal rules that govern their behavior. When the statutory text clearly answers the interpretive question, therefore, it normally will be the most important consideration. Exceptions, however, do exist because an apparently clear text can be rendered ambiguous by a demonstration of contrary legislative expectations or highly unreasonable consequences. The historical perspective is the next most important interpretive consideration; given the traditional assumptions that the legislature is the supreme lawmaking body in a democracy, the historical expectations of the enacting legislature are entitled to deference. Hence, when a clear text and supportive legislative history suggest the same answer, they typically will control.

The dynamic model, however, views the evolutive perspective as most important when the statutory text is not clear and the original legislative expectations have been overtaken by subsequent changes in society and law. In such cases, the pull of text and history will be slight, and the interpreter will find current policies and societal conditions most important. The hardest cases, obviously, are those in which a clear text or strong historical evidence or both, are inconsistent with compelling current values and policies.

William N. Eskridge, Jr., Dynamic Statutory Interpretation, 135 U. Pa. L. Rev. 1479, 1482-1484 (1987). A clear example of what Professor Eskridge would consider a dynamic interpretation is Justice Blackmun's view of the applicability of Title VII of the Civil Rights Act of 1964, expressed in United States Steelworkers of America, AFL-CIO-CLC v. Weber (see page 16).

As noted above, these "new canons" do not describe (except perhaps for Professor Eskridge's view) what the courts actually do, but outline theories of interpretation that their proponents would like to debate and see adopted. From this perspective, on what basis can a court adopt such "new" canons? As Justice Breyer has observed:

Can the Court legally adopt new up-to-date canons, such as those Professor Sunstein has suggested? . . . [C]an the Court simply adopt them? Where would it find the legal authority for

doing so? Unlike the older canons, these new canons lack the
legitimacy provided by continuous judicial use over many
years. The traditional canons may seem out-of-date, but they
possess a time-honored acceptance that newer, up-to-date
canons lack.

Stephen Breyer, On the Uses of Legislative History in
Interpreting Statutes, 65 S. Cal. L. Rev. 845, 870 (1992). Indeed,
as Professor Ross points out, these canons are not intended to
"describe accurately what Congress actually intended or what
the words of a statute mean, but rather to direct courts to construe any ambiguity in a particular way in order to further
some policy objective." Stephen Ross, Where Have You Gone,
Karl Llewellyn? Should Congress Turn Its Lonely Eyes to
You?, 45 Vand. L. Rev. 561, 563 (1992). Of course, the practical
significance of these new canons awaits judicial response in
prospective cases.

D.   THE INTERPRETATION OF LAW
ENACTED THROUGH INITIATIVE
AND REFERENDUM

In the sections above, we have discussed the interpretation
of statutes enacted through the legislative process. Not all
statutes are enacted in that fashion. For example, law students
and lawyers in California quite regularly are required to interpret statutes enacted through an initiative process. Today
some 20 states have direct initiative processes that allow
citizens to initiate and enact legislation, totally bypassing their
state legislatures. Some additional states have a form of
initiative that gives the legislature an opportunity to enact the
initiated legislation. If the legislation is not enacted within a
specific time period, it then goes to referendum.

Since the 1970s, initiatives have addressed subjects as diverse as public morality, governmental processes, taxation, labor regulation, business regulation, utility rates, zoning and
land use, health, welfare reform, housing, homelessness, education, civil rights, environmental protection, and nuclear
power. During the early 1990s, the most noted initiatives were
a California effort to limit the rights of illegal aliens and their

children, a California effort to prohibit affirmative actions, the efforts of several states to restrict the rights of homosexuals, and Oregon's doctor-assisted suicide law.

Initiative refers to the process of having legislation (or constitutional amendments) placed directly on the ballot, usually through a petitioning process, and then voted on by the public. A modified form of this process (sometimes referred to as an *indirect initiative*) uses the petitioning process to trigger legislative consideration of a particular proposal. Such a proposal is only subject to referendum in the event that the legislature does not adopt it. *Referendum* refers to the process by which legislative enactments are required to be approved by the electorate before they can become effective. In some states, particular types of legislation (for example, creating debt) must be subject to referendum. Another form of referendum allows the public, through a petitioning process, to require an enacted bill to be submitted to the voters.

The frequent use of initiatives since the 1970s has led to considerable debate about their efficacy. This debate has basically addressed two issues: (1) how successful initiatives have been as measured against their goals, and (2) how they compare as a lawmaking process with representative democracy. A debate is also rising over their constitutional validity. For a discussion of this debate, see Abner J. Mikva and Eric Lane, Legislative Process (1995). For a recent case declaring a particular initiative violative of the Constitution's Equal Protection Clause, see Romer v. Evans, 116 S. Ct. 1620 (1996).

The increasingly frequent use of initiatives raises another important question about their statutory product: How are they to be interpreted? The application of such statutes produces the same problems of "meaning" as legislative-enacted statutes, but are these problems susceptible to the same interpretive approaches used in the interpretation of legislative law? More particularly, if the language of the statute does not provide an answer to the question under litigation, what sources of meaning are available to provide an answer? As Professor Jane S. Schacter, in her significant article about the interpretation of initiatives, has written:

> Consider, for example, the mass size of the electorate; the absence of legislative hearings, committee reports, or other recorded legislative history; and the inability of citizen lawmakers

to deliberate about, or to amend proposed ballot measures. In addition, voters are not professional lawmakers so it is problematic to impute to the electorate the same knowledge about law, legal terminology, and legislative context that courts routinely ascribe — if sometimes only as aspiration — to legislators.

Jane S. Schacter, The Pursuit of "Popular Intent": Interpretive Dilemmas in Direct Democracy, 105 Yale L.J. 107, 110 (1995).

Aside from the work of Professor Schacter, little scholarly attention has focused on this problem, and we rely heavily on her work to describe the approaches most courts have adopted. According to Schacter, "courts widely subject citizen-lawmakers to the same standards as legislators and generally confine their search to sources commonly used in construing legislative law," despite the fact that the interpretive sources for initiative laws might "differ from those used in construing legislative law because of, for example, the absence of a legislative record and the fact that voters are not professional." Id. at 119-120. For example, in their search for the meaning of a provision in an initiative law, courts have relied on "popular intent" (as analogy to legislative intent), drawn from the same sources used for legislative law: the statute's language, the body of existing law and its legislative history, legal text, judicial and administrative decisions, and canons of construction.

This reliance on a traditional methodology is to be expected. The language of the initiative, read or not read, understood or not understood, is that which is enacted. If it is ambiguous, the courts' search for the law's meaning in traditional sources, along with ballot material, would seem natural. But such approaches require careful analysis. Professor Schacter, for example, is very critical, arguing that interpretive rules consistent with characteristics of the initiative process need to judicially framed.

CHAPTER TWO.

The Legislative Process

In this chapter we look broadly at the legislative process. Our focus is not on the detail of the process, which comes in Chapter 3, but on its characteristics, structures, and rules. We start with a description of the "real" legislative process, then follow with some brief observations about the functions of American legislatures and two of their often overlooked highlights: compromise and executive involvement. Next we explore the three main legitimizing characteristics of the legislative process: representativeness, accessibility, and deliberativeness. Following that, we turn our attention to legislative structures and their roles in the legislative process. Finally, we end with a discussion of legislative rules and their enforcement.

Familiarity with the legislative process (including its structure) is essential to the modern lawyer. Knowledge of the process is an obvious requirement for monitoring statutory development or for representing a client before a legislative body.

Familiarity with the legislative process is also necessary for statutory interpretation. Some points of this nexus are evident. When the court or an attorney explores a statute's legislative history they are opening a window on the enactment process and must be able to appreciate what they see. Also, as we noted in Chapter One, every statute has its own legislative history that must be explored in searching for the meaning of the particular statutory language in question.

Similarly, the use of canons of interpretation import the lawmaking process into the interpretive process. Canons, as we discussed in Chapter 1, are general presumptions about legislative intent and process. As also noted earlier, one of the most substantial criticisms of their use is that as general propositions about legislative intent they are wrong because they misread the legislative process. For example, use of the canon that remedial statutes should be read broadly might be tempered by an understanding that legislative process is one of compromises. Understanding that compromise is an essential part of the legislative process should provide several lessons for interpreters, particularly for controversial legislation. Professor John Copeland Nagle names two: "many questions are left unanswered and no goal is pursued at all costs." John Copeland Nagle, CERCLA's Mistakes, 38 Wm. & Mary L. Rev. 1405 (1997). This first lesson, of course, offers one reason why much legislation is subject to appellate litigation and suggests that not every litigated question will have a legislative answer — the hard cases of interpretation discussed in Chapter One, section B4. The second lesson is important in understanding a statute's purpose. Appreciation of this lesson might have tempered Justice Brennan's view in United Steelworkers of America, AFL-CIO-CLC v. Weber, as discussed in Chapter One, pages 14-16.

Finally, judicial views of the legislative process are part of the mix that result in a judicial decision. Judge Posner makes this point aptly:

> The point is general. The interpretation of statutes is highly sensitive to theories of the legislative process, and these are controversial political theories and hence do not provide sure footing for judicial decisions. Those who believe that legislatures embody the popular will and who venerate popular democracy are likely to attach great weight to any indications of how a majority of the legislature might have answered the interpretive question that has arisen. Those who regard the impediments to the legislative process as salutary checks on the excesses of democracy are likely to be distrustful of any expressions of legislative preference that have not run the gauntlet. There is no basis in law — maybe no basis period, in current political theory— for choosing between these positions. Interpretation is not foundational; it sits uneasily on shifting political foundations.

Richard A. Posner, The Problems of Jurisprudence 292 (1990). Judge Posner's observation is well evidenced by debate over the use of legislative history in the interpretation of statutes. Justice Scalia's skepticism over the integrity of the legislative process, among other things, results in his determination to avoid its use. This debate is described in section B3b of Chapter One. Similarly, Judge Easterbrook's narrow approach to interpretation is based on a view that the legislative process is one of "deal cutting." On the other hand, Justice Breyer's support for the use of legislative history may be partially explained by his favorable experience as Counsel to the Senate Judiciary Committee. And finally, Professor Eskridge's "dynamic" approach, in part, sees the legislative process as too slow and cumbersome to maintain current policies and values in law. The goal of this chapter is to introduce the legislative process. We emphasize the word *introduce*. A full picture is beyond our present scope. For a more detailed look, see Abner J. Mikva and Eric Lane, Legislative Process (1995), and sources noted therein.

A.   THE "REAL" LEGISLATIVE PROCESS

In outline, the legislative process seems elementary and familiar. Legislators are elected. Legislators introduce proposed laws in the form of a bill. The bill is sent to a committee. If adopted by the committee, with or without amendments, it usually reaches the floor of the legislature. If passed there, the bill is sent to the other legislative house (the federal and all state governments except Nebraska have bicameral legislatures), where the same process occurs. If the second house passes the bill in the identical form passed by the first house, it is sent to the executive. The executive either approves the bill (making it law) or vetoes the bill. If vetoed, the bill is sent back to the legislature, which can override the veto by a supermajority.

Such a description of the legislative process, while accurate, is not revealing. It misses the complex structures and processes through which an enacted statute is really shaped. As President, then Professor, Woodrow Wilson wrote:

> Like a vast picture thronged with figures of equal prominence and crowded with elaborate and obtrusive details, Congress is hard to see satisfactorily and appreciatively at a single view and from a single stand-point. Its complicated forms and diversified structure confuse the vision, and conceal the system which

underlies its composition. It is too complex to be understood without an effort, without a careful and systematic process of analysis.

Woodrow Wilson, Congressional Government 57 (Johns Hopkins Univ. Press ed. 1981).

The following description of New York State's legislative process illustrates President Wilson's observation. In reading this description, consider the various procedural difficulties that must be overcome to enact legislation. Missing from this description is any reference to the executive's role in the enactment process, which is discussed in section A3 of this chapter and in Chapter Three. The New York legislative process described below is one the nation's least deliberative. See Eric Lane, Albany's Travesty of Democracy, City Journal 49 (Spring 1997). A description of most other states' legislative processes would show even more complication and diversification.

ERIC LANE, LEGISLATIVE PROCESS AND ITS JUDICIAL RENDERINGS
48 U. Pitt. L. Rev. 639, 645-650 (1987)

[Introduction of Legislation]

Ideas for the introduction of bills spring from many sources, including constituents, lobbyists, representatives of other governmental agencies, as well as from the legislator's own perception of district and state problems needing legislative response. The decision to propose legislation is related of course to the demand level, the legislator's own interest in and concern about the subject, and his or her own level of legislative industriousness. The more complicated a legislative solution appears to be, the fewer the number of members willing to undertake it.

[Drafting Legislation]

In most cases, once the decision to introduce legislation has been made, the outline of a legislative response will be drafted. That response generally will be a joint effort of the legislator, legislative staff and, in many cases, interest groups which favor the measure. . . . [T]his legislative outline will [in many jurisdictions] then be forwarded to a bill drafter. . . .

The bill drafter is responsible for transforming the proposed solution into bill language, bill form, and to fit its provision within the existing body of statutory law. A draft bill is then produced and returned to the requesting legislator for review. The main purpose of this review is to make sure that the bill drafter has properly translated the legislator's ideas. Revisions, if needed, are then made and the bill is introduced. . . .

Many bills, however, follow different paths to introduction. A member will sometimes introduce a bill provided by the executive or an outside group. On other occasions, depending on the significance of the problem to the particular legislator and the sophistication of the legislator's staff, the bill will be drafted by the legislator and his or her staff. In certain instances bills will also be drafted by the staff [of a relevant committee or] of the conference to which the legislator belongs. This latter category always includes the session's most controversial bills and also frequently involves bills on issues on which the [committee or] conference staff has developed particular expertise. . . .

[Committees]

Once a bill has been introduced, it is referred to a committee where the vast majority of bills are gratefully allowed to die. For example, of the 9,624 bills introduced in the New York State Senate in 1986, only 1,852 bills passed the Senate, while only 265 bills were actually signed into law. One reason for this disparity is that in New York, unlike some other states, a member may introduce an unlimited number of bills. Consequently, legislators will introduce legislation in response to almost any demand from constituents, lobbyists or other interest groups. The introduction of legislation, thus, is frequently not a commitment to pursuing passage of a new law or even airing a proposal, but rather a tactic for reducing pressure from these groups.

[Majority Building]

Once a "serious" bill is referred to a committee, two overlapping processes begin, revision and majority building. The revision process, in its most limited sense, is the process by which a bill is reviewed by committee members, staff and conference staff to ensure that the legislative idea is properly expressed. This process continues even after a bill has been reported from the committee to the legislative calendar. Not infrequently, a bill will pass through several prints prior to the actual vote on it. A bill will also undergo revisions in the process of building a majority as provisions are changed to secure the number of votes needed for passage.

[Noncontroversial Bills]

The process of building a majority in the New York State Legislature is relatively easy for most bills. In New York, as in all other states, the legislature has jurisdiction over numerous local matters such as alienating public property, creating municipal water districts, and other similar matters. As a result, a large number of bills are not controversial and they occasion no particular contention. These local bills generally pass the legislature with near unanimity, and with very little individual legislative attention other than that of the sponsor. Legislative staff members, however, will generally review those bills to verify their clarity and provide summaries of their contents to the conference members. Local bills tend to generate little litigation.

Bills other than local bills may also be noncontroversial. Whether a bill is noncontroversial or controversial depends not on the significance of a bill's content, but on the intensity and diversity of the legislative viewpoints which swirl around its contents. For example, a corporate take-over bill enacted in 1985, the contents of which had potentially profound effects on the New York economy, sailed through the legislative process virtually without comment. As with local bills, the absence of legislative contention concerning potentially significant legislation means that the bill will receive less legislative attention, although a significant bill will generate extensive staff-prepared briefing papers.

[Controversial Bills]

While bills for which it is difficult to build a majority are far fewer in number, they take up the largest part of legislative time. These are the controversial bills, which, to repeat, are not defined by their content but by the intensity and diversity of the legislative viewpoints with which they are received. The intensity and variety of legislative viewpoints that a bill generates are of course fueled by a mixture of influences including individual and party policy, political predilections, and constituency and interest group pressures. The more intense and diverse the viewpoints and hence the more controversial a bill is, the more the legislative body will focus on the particular subject of the bill and strain to void that irritant. During this period of strain, legislative politics is at its most robust and fragile and "essential techniques of politics in real life persuasion, exchange of services, rewards and benefits, alliances and deals" take place. In addition, during this time the legislative process exercises its most moderating influence on those with inconsistent viewpoints, as compromises are forged to win votes and reduce adverse pressures. While this process frequently does not allow for an individual drafter to explore every implication of a bill, the foreseeable implications are generally examined in the intense exchanges which occur among interested parties, through which the ultimate legislation is fashioned.

[Party Conferences]

Majorities are most frequently built before a bill is ready for formal legislative action. In the New York State Legislature, majority building generally occurs in private nonrecorded conferences, where legislative leaders express their views on bills, staff are given an opportunity to fully brief the legislators on the provisions of each controversial bill, members most openly discuss the policies and politics of each bill, and conference negotiators are given their instructions. The more controversial a bill becomes, the more it will be discussed in conference and the less freedom negotiators will have in making an agreement. . . .

Legislative conferences also bring together members of the same party for intra-party trading. Inter-party trading and discussions with lobbyists, of course, occur outside the conference, although the results of this trading are brought inside by the actions of the particular legislator with respect to controversial legislation.

[Floor Debates]

Since most majorities are built behind the scenes, it is rare for a floor debate to influence the outcome of a bill, particularly a controversial one. As a result, most statements on the floor do not relate to the deliberative process, but to the public relations process. In other words, members do not speak substantively to their colleagues in floor debate, but politically to their constituents and interest groups. Occasionally, however, there will be an actual floor debate in which an analysis of the bill is undertaken. This debate will almost always involve the bill's sponsor and presents one of the few publicly accessible moments of actual legislative deliberation or exposition. . . .

[The Legislative Decision]

While the decision to support or oppose a noncontroversial bill is rather simple, grounded to a large extent in personal affinities and leadership cues, the decision on a controversial bill is more complex. The more controversial a bill, the more the typical legislator's decision will be the product of his or her independent cognitive process. This process of deciding whether to support or oppose a controversial bill will include the legislator's own understanding of a bill based on a reading of it, a reading of staff-prepared memoranda, and discussion with colleagues and lobbyists. Contrary to what has been suggested by some critics, legislators are generally familiar with the particulars of controversial legislation which they enact. Once a bill is understood, numerous factors are weighed in determining whether to vote for its enactment. They include the legislator's judgment on the merits of the bill, the views of his or her constituents, any impact on the chances of reelection, views of lobbyists and colleagues, conference and leadership views of editorial boards, campaign fund-raising opportunities, opportunities for amending the proposed legislation, and opportunities for trading for the support of his or her own legislation or for other legislative favors. It is impossible to determine in any given case the weight of any of these factors, since they depend to a large extent on the continuing intensity of each and on the current needs of the legislator.

The significance of Professor Lane's description is not its particular detailing of the New York State legislative process.

Such details may vary from jurisdiction to jurisdiction and from time to time. For example, in Congress there may be more emphasis on the committees and less on leadership (although not in the first years of the Gingrich Speakership, 1995-1996, during which we write) or more on floor debate and less on party conferences. Rather, the description's importance is its portrayal of the complexity of the legislative structures and processes and the difficulty experienced in converting most ideas, particularly controversial ones, into law. These difficulties are a hallmark of American legislative process and one of its legitimizing characteristics. (See section B of this chapter.)

1.   What American Legislatures Do

We started this book by noting that we live in an age of statutes. We defined this age as one in which statutes dominate the legal landscape either through direct regulation and redistribution or as the basis for the regulatory authority of administrative agencies. From this perspective, the function of legislatures may be seen simply as the enactment of laws. Statutes, as we also observed earlier, are not abstract. They are produced through demand, pursued and screened through the legislative process. The age of statutes, then, includes the intense competition among broad arrays of interest groups to have their interests shape political agendas and the law. As described by the legal historian Willard Hurst, "Legislation bulked larger in social regulation when more numerous and varied interests began to press claims for attention, and when politically effective opinion sensed a need to bring more factors into policy calculations. In that context both petitioners and lawmakers began to realize the process implications of the open-door jurisdiction of the legislative branch in contrast to the narrower avenues of access to judicial lawmaking." J. Willard Hurst, Dealing with Statutes 12 (1982). From this perspective, the function of legislatures is far more complex. It is in the legislative arena, through use of its processes, that the fierce battles between groups occur and are resolved. It is through the legislative process that group demands, first, may be recognized as problems that require legislative attention and, second, may be accommodated through legislation. Key to any such accommodation is the legislative compromise through which the views of competing groups and of legislators are all tempered and blended together into a statute.

The significance of the compromise to the legislative process is discussed in the next section. The different aspects of the legislative process are the subjects of section C of this chapter. What needs emphasis in this section for the interpretation and understanding of statutes is that, unlike the judicial system with its focus on the rightness or wrongness of individual acts in the context of some governing law, the focus of the legislative process is on the identification of problems and the melding of competing views about these problems into politically and substantively acceptable solutions.

2.   *The Importance of Compromise*

Mythic is the person who stands on principle alone, but in the legislative arena, the moderation of policy preference is not viewed as a fall from virtue. In many cases, it is considered virue, if such moderation leads to legislative progress. While compromise sometimes leads to criticism of the legislative process, compromise is one of its major goals, and it is only through compromise that problems are addressed. This is a consequence of the structure and process of American legislatures, which make it practically impossible for bills to become laws without compromise. For a bill to become law, it must, constitutionally, win the majority of votes in each house of a legislature, or more votes, if the executive exercises veto power. It must also, in most cases, first win the votes of a variety of legislative committees before it can ever reach the legislative floor. To win a committee majority and a house majority in each legislative house, a bill must be acceptable to a substantial number of legislators, many of whom have different views of the problem and the solution the bill addresses.

Compromise is also a consequence of meeting in assembly. As legislators become increasingly familiar with each other, they become more and more familiar and comfortable with each others' views and interests. In short, they come to appreciate other policy views and interests. Former Speaker of

the New York State Assembly Stanley Fink describes this
process during an interview in which he talks about his first
year in office.

> I went to Albany as a New York City representative, to pursue
> an urban agenda. But through formal and informal interactions
> with my colleagues across the state, I began to recognize and
> appreciate the views and interests of representatives from other
> areas. The result of this education was that my advocacy for ur-
> ban interests was frequently tempered by my understanding of
> its impact on the interest of others.

The importance of compromise to the process places a
premium on the political skills of its participants. While rational argument remains an important currency, the ability to
negotiate and moderate views in the context of such negotiation is equally important. From a legislative perspective "half a
loaf" is almost always better than none.

3.   The Executive as Legislator

The focus of this chapter and the next is primarily on the
legislative process as performed by legislators in a legislative
body. But no discussion of the legislative process should fail to
note the central and pervasive role that the president and
states governors play in the consideration of legislation. So significant has this role been at times that one political scientist
writes (though perhaps overstated): "The legislature is not the
dominant influence in the legislative process. The President is
more influential. He leads and Congress controls. Leadership
in this context means two things: to initiate the legislative
process, that is to perform its early stages, and to impel it, or to
continuously drive its process forward." Arthur Maas, Congress and the Common Good 10 (1983).

This role for the nation's executives is not portrayed
through a literal reading of the U.S. or state constitutions. The
veto power (see Chapter Three, section C13) that the president
and all of the states' executives (except North Carolina's)
enjoy, of course, provides some executive leverage. A veto
changes the vote needed to pass legislation and creates a
different political dynamic in which legislation is considered.

The threat of veto opens legislative doors to executive participation in many cases in which he or she would not otherwise be welcome. But it is not the veto alone that accounts for such widespread executive participation. Nor do the provisions in the U.S. Constitution and state constitutions that require executives to report on the state of the union and recommend measures (see, for example, Article 2, §3 of the U.S. Constitution) explain executive participation. Although these provisions provide the constitutional imprimatur for executives' state of the union messages and an active executive legislative role, the energy for executive action flows from living in an age of statutes and the consequential political process in which the executive, as the nation's or state's leader, is seen by the public as the most important initiator of legislation. This is underscored by election campaigns that generally revolve around ideas for legislation. The Voting Rights Act of 1965, discussed later in this chapter and in Chapter Three, was a presidential initiative and probably would not have become law without the executive efforts to mobilize the nation in its support.

B.   WHAT MAKES THE LEGISLATIVE PROCESS LEGITIMATE?

On page 55, we included Judge Posner's observation that approaches to statutory interpretation are based, at least in part, on judicial views of the legislative process. While we cannot measure the prevalence or dominance of this perspective, it is certainly an important part of the mix. A judge's view of the legitimacy of the legislative process generally, or particularly in the case of a single statute, is a factor in that judge's sense of obligation to obey a statutory command, his or her evaluation of a statute's clarity, and his or her attitude toward legislative history. Justice Scalia's abhorrence and Justice Breyer's embrace of legislative history, discussed in Chapter One, well illustrates the point.

The legitimacy of the legislative process is not just a factor in the judicial application of statutes. The success of a representative democracy requires a public sense of legitimacy in the efforts of representative bodies. This is particularly true in the age of statutes, in which a vast array of varied interest groups fiercely compete in legislative arenas to have their interests prevail. The legislative function is to determine which views merit consideration and how they should be accommodated. But this function must be effected in a manner that maintains public confidence in the fairness or legitimacy of the system.

The legitimacy of the American legislative process is intended to derive from its three salient characteristics: deliberativeness, representativeness, and accessibility. Although forged by the Framers as a result of their fear of centralized power and individual and group self-interest, the details of these characteristics are not set in stone. They have followed the many changes in attitudes and policies of the nation and have been crafted in the nation's political ovens. But these changes have not, nor could they have, insulated the legislative process from criticism. Today, as throughout our history, the process remains the subject of constant critical exploration. The purpose of this section is to introduce each of these legitimizing characteristics and to explore briefly the major issues that impact on their effectiveness in legitimizing the actions of American legislatures.

1.   Deliberativeness

Earlier in this chapter, we described the difficulties encountered in the enactment of legislation as a unique hallmark of the American legislative process. Such difficulties are the intended consequence of the deliberative characteristic of the American legislative process. Deliberativeness is not a synonym for debate, although debate may be one of its elements. Rather, the term defines those structures and steps of the legislative process (for example, bicameralism and the executive veto) that slow legislative decision making and distance it from the passions and immediacy of the prevailing desires of individual legislators and of various constituencies. "If men were angels, no government would be necessary. If angels were to govern men neither external nor internal controls on government would be necessary," wrote James Madison in The Federalist No. 51. But since men and women were not seen as angels, but as zealous advocates for a vast array of differing and competing interests, the Framers adopted a form of government intended for the control of the various and conflicting interests that competed for favorable governmental treatment. Representativeness (discussed in the following section) is one such vehicle for the regulation of competing interests. But to block the opportunity for individual legislators or small groups of legislators to determine the outcome of the legislative process, the Framers established a bicameral legislative body, with both different modes of election and a substantial executive role through possession of the veto power.

Each phase of the enactment process creates a point at which a bill's progress can be delayed or halted. Advancement requires support from varying numbers of legislative colleagues or coalitions of colleagues, almost none of whom share each others' exact ideas, concerns, or constituencies. This is particularly true in Congress, whose members represent the entire diversity of the nation. Winning such support can result from numerous factors, including persuasive debate, compromises, favors, trades, and political force. Such activity is complicated, difficult to observe, and hard to digest. (From this flows the often quoted multisourced simile comparing the legislative process to sausage-making.)

The deliberativeness of the legislative process has engendered considerable criticism. Characterizing the process as gridlocked, critics argue for reforms to make the process more efficient or to circumvent the process, for example, through initiative and referendum. Numerous polls also indicate public skepticism over the ability of government to do the right thing. The legitimacy of American government also depends on its ability to recognize and respond to serious problems. But, while it may be argued that modern expectations of the role of government and unceasing demands for governmental solutions to problems require more efficient models than those offered by our present system, it can be similarly argued that, in the face of such expectations and demands, the need for deliberativeness and consensus is all the more acute.

2. *Representativeness*

American democracy is representative. This means that a small number of elected officials are delegated the authority to enact laws, in assembly. This choice is not abstract. Through representative democracy the Framers intended, among other things, to create a system through which public views could be considered and refined and through which the passions of majority factions could be tempered. The legitimacy of a representative democracy flows from two factors: public satisfaction with the breadth of suffrage and with the definition of the representative relationship. Few people, for example, would consider the efforts of a legislature elected only by white male property owners legitimate. Of course, the franchise now is far broader, and, after the centuries of struggle, most issues about suffrage have been resolved. Article XIX of the U.S. Constitution (1920) assured female suffrage. And the Voting Rights Act of 1965 and its 1970, 1975, and 1982 amendments have basically assured a full voting franchise for African Americans, Latinos, and other minorities.

Underlying attention to the electorate as a measure of legislative legitimacy is the basic premise that, in a representative democracy, "[e]lections provide the chief means through which most voters influence the formation of government policy and exercise the right responsibilities of citizenship." A. James Reichley, The Electoral System, in Elections American Style 1, 1 (1987). It is primarily through elections that the public exercises power over the legislative process and the behavior of its elected representatives. It is also through elections that the public's views begin their path to becoming public policy.

For candidates, of course, elections are the way they become and remain legislators. As the political scientist David Mayhew has observed about members of Congress, "[r]eelection underlies everything else, as indeed it should, if we are to expect that the relation between politicians and public will be one of accountability." David R. Mayhew, The Electoral Connection and the Congress, reprinted in Congress: Structure and Policy 19 (Mathew D. McCubbins and Terry Sullivan eds., 1987). As might be expected, the connection between election and the behavior of legislators is the subject of considerable study by political scientists, and it is one we touch on a number of times in this book. The general view (one that the authors share based on their experience) is that while reelection is extremely important to legislators, for most it is not their sole goal nor their sole consideration, but a means for them to accomplish their other goals.

The election of legislators raises some thorny questions. Philosophically, there is the question of how much duty the legislator owes to the wishes of his or her constituents. Politically, there is the almost unresolvable question of how a legislator is to meet conflicting public demands that he or she simultaneously rise above the political fray and also serve as advocate of local interests. Finally, there is the particularly current question of the impact of campaign financing on the legislative function.

a.   What Is the Duty of a Representative

Central to an understanding of the role of the legislator in the legislative process is the concept of the representative relationship between the representative and his or her constituents. The nature of this relationship was the subject of considerable attention and controversy during the debate over the ratification of the Constitution. The debate continues today among political scientists and ethicists. It is confusion about this relationship that also underlies much of the criticism of legislators as the public either wants them to ignore district interests, for the public interest, or to pay attention to district interests, as the district's representative.

The debate revolves around the question of what is and what ought to be the duty of an elected representative. Answers range from acting pursuant to the wishes of a majority of constituents (the delegate theory) to acting pursuant to his or her best judgment or conscience (the trustee theory). According to Professor Gordon Wood, the concept of an "instructed" representative is consistent with founding American experience, however impractical or philosophically unsavory this idea may have become. Gordon Wood, The Creation of the American Republic, 1776-1787, 162-175 (1969).

But this debate only provides some guideposts for understanding representation. The legislative process is too complex and the rational need for compromise too great to permit neat categories. Nor are most issues susceptible to such categorization. A legislator may have a variety of allegiances, concerns, and sensibilities on any given issue that he or she factors into the making of a particular decision. What can be observed is that, for the most part, legislators reflect the dominant attitudes and status of their constituents and believe they are responsible for expressing the same in the legislative arena. In the experience of both of the authors, legislators first respond to proposed legislation on the basis of their own policy views and then, where appropriate, refract them through other relevant prisms, such as constituent and party demands. The basis on which a decision is made depends on the intensity of each factor.

Sometimes legislators actually do join issue at the extremes of this debate. This arises when an issue, such as abortion or the death penalty, becomes so poignant that it touches a legislator's personal sense of morality. A more frequent example of a voting dilemma is the choice between an obvious local interest and an obvious national interest. Extreme examples of this are votes on the closing of military bases or votes adversely affecting the tobacco industry by representatives from tobacco producing states. In each case, successful legislation may cause substantial economic disruption to the legislator's district and raise serious campaign issues. Consider the comments of Senator Robert C. Byrd of West Virginia explaining his opposition to an otherwise broadly supported clean air bill, which passed the Senate by a vote of 89-11: "I cannot vote for legislation that can bring economic ruin to communities throughout the Appalachian region and the Midwest." N.Y. Times, Apr. 4, 1990, at A20. Senator Byrd had unsuccessfully advocated an appropriation for support of mine workers who would lose their jobs as a result of the limitations on the production of high sulphur coal. During this same period of time, Representative Byron Dorgan of North Dakota was winning praise for opposing construction in his district of part of the MX missile system. Despite the fact that the installation represented a multimillion dollar investment in his district, Dorgan argued "[t]o those in my district who yearn for the economic activity generated by the MX program . . . I must say that's not the economic activity that builds a better future for us and our children." N.Y. Times, Mar. 31, 1990, at A24.

b.   The Impact of Campaign Financing on
the Representative

While it is likely that the above debate will remain chronic and unresolved with little impact on legislative legitimacy, one question of representativeness that emerges more and more as a challenge to legislative legitimacy is the impact of campaign fund-raising on the representative relationship.

Campaigns for legislative office cost money. Money enables the candidates to wage their campaigns, and it is through this money that they inform the public of their candidacy. As Professor Herbert Alexander, one of the nation's leading campaign finance scholars has remarked, "Money, lots of it, is essential to the smooth conduct of our system of free elections." Herbert E. Alexander, Financing Politics 1 (3d ed. 1984).

This need for money has exploded in recent decades. Increased dependency on electronic media and the decline of political party strength have dramatically increased the cost of campaigns. This has resulted in an enormous increase in the amount of time, energy, and resources that candidates (including incumbents) must dedicate to fund-raising and has placed a premium on individual wealth as a factor in candidate selection. This search for campaign money, at times almost hysterical, has had a negative impact on public attitudes toward the political process. The more that candidates search for money, the more the public believes that contributions influence their policy views. This skepticism undermines the legitimacy of legislative policy making.

Historically, Congress has not simply stood on the sidelines and watched this erosion of its own public image. In 1974, it enacted the Federal Election Campaign Act Amendments of 1974 (FECA) to limit the press for money in federal elections. At the heart of this statute for congressional candidates were limitations on both campaign contributions and expenditures and requirements for broad disclosure. For presidential campaigns, the statute established a voluntary public financing program. The full effect of this statute was short lived. In 1976 the U.S. Supreme Court declared in Buckley v. Valeo, 424 U.S. 1 (1976), that the act's limits on candidates' expenditure from their own personal funds and on overall campaign expenditures violated the First Amendment's guarantee of free political expression. The Court left intact the acts' limitation on contributions ($1000 by individuals, $5000 by political committees) and its required disclosure procedures. According to the Court, "the amount of money a person or group can spend on political communication during a campaign necessarily reduces the quantity of expression by restricting the number of issues discussed, the depth of their exploration, and the size of the audience reached." 424 U.S. at 19. On the other hand, the Court saw contribution limits as a more marginal restriction on political speech because the contribution "does not communicate the basis for the support [for] [the political message]. The quantity of communication by the contributor does not increase perceptibly with the size of his contribution, since the expression rests solely on the undifferentiated, symbolic act of contributing. At most, the size of the contribution provides a very rough index of the intensity of the contributor's support for the candidate." Id. at 21. The Court did leave open the possibility that too severe a limitation to contributions could have the effect of restricting political speech if such limitations "prevented candidates . . . from amassing the resources necessary for effective advocacy." Id. at 21.

FECA, as modified by the *Buckley* decision, has not been without its virtues. The public disclosure rules have provided a picture of congressional contributors, and the contribution limits have reduced the importance of "fat cats" and created broader fund-raising bases.

But what these reforms have not been able to accomplish, because of *Buckley*, is a limitation on the costs of campaigns, which has resulted in increased pressure on candidates to raise money, and a limitation on personal expenditures that have allowed rich candidates to have extraordinary advantages over other candidates. These pressures have also been increased by inflation, which has substantially eroded the buying power of the $1000 limit on individual contribution. Together these factors have created a demand for additional sources of money, which has been addressed, to some extent, by the rise of political action committees (PACs) and the use of numerous loopholes in the law to circumvent spending limits, for example, one allowing basically unlimited contributions (soft money) to political parties that run, theoretically, independent campaigns for candidates of their selection.

The rising costs of congressional campaigns (one product of Buckley v. Valeo) and the consequential intensifying search by candidates for more and more contributions raise a number of problematic issues. First, public skepticism about the electoral process is growing as fund-raising increasingly dominates election efforts. Such skepticism undermines the legitimacy of representative lawmaking. Doubts about the legitimacy of the legislative process are important factors in, for example, the term limit efforts and the growing use of initiatives and referenda. Second, competitive elections are harder and harder to mount, and personal wealth is now a major factor in determining challenger candidacies. Third, fund-raising gobbles up excessive amounts of time that incumbent candidates could use for their legislative work or that all candidates could use to focus on public issues.

Concern over all of these issues continues pressure on Congress to reform the campaign finance system. While numerous reform bills have been introduced, no substantial reforms have been enacted. To some extent this failure has been the product of incumbency politics, as meaningful reform would benefit challengers. But, to a large extent, the reform task has been burdened by the limits established by the *Buckley* decision. Simply put, if the problem is the cost of campaigns and if expenditures cannot be directly limited, how can the problem be resolved?

One approach is to reduce existing contribution limits. This approach, of course, does nothing to solve the problem of campaign costs and probably adds to the already heavy fund-raising pressure. At some point the limitation on contributions may also run into First Amendment problems under the theory that restriction on right of individuals to contribute is too onerous. See, for example, Day v. Hayes, 863 F. Supp. 940, *aff'd*, 34 F.3d 1356 (8th Cir. 1994). (D. Minn. 1994) (invalidating $100 contribution limit). Another set of proposals focuses on eliminating or further restricting PACs.

More comprehensive approaches focus on the costs of campaigns and attempt to find ways to circumvent *Buckley*'s restrictions. Most prominent among these are the establishment of spending limits with public funds or resources, in

some form, as an incentive for conformity. A number of scholars also are attempting to create a stronger doctrinal justification for expenditure limitations in the hope that Congress may
revisit this approach, despite *Buckley*'s determination of their
unconstitutionality.

3.   *Accessibility (with a Particular Look at Lobbying)*

The third legitimizing characteristic of American legislatures is accessibility. Representative government requires public accessibility to insure its accountability and integrity.

Accessibility includes the right of people to know what
their legislators are doing (and not doing) in the conduct of
public business. This was underscored early in our history by
James Madison when he wrote, "A popular government, without popular information, or the means of acquiring it, is but a
prologue to a farce or a tragedy, or perhaps both." Letter from
James Madison to W. T. Barby, Aug. 4, 1822, in 9 Writings of
James Madison at 103 (Hunt ed. 1910). This "right to know" is
formalized in constitutions and statutes that require, for example, public notice of prospective legislative meetings and
legislation, the maintenance of public journals of legislative
votes, and open legislative meetings. Many of these requisites
have been hard won against the opposition of legislators. Legislators have been reluctant to open their processes to public
view, believing in part that too much openness impedes the
necessary process of compromise, militates against legislative
effectiveness, and may injure their reelection opportunities.

These openness requirements, which vary from jurisdiction to jurisdiction, focus on the formal steps of law making:
the introduction of legislation, consideration of legislation by
both committees (at hearings or in meetings) and the legislative body, and any final outcome of any such consideration.
But advocacy and the exchange of information in the legislative process, unlike the judicial process, are not restricted to
formal, recorded settings at which all interested parties are
present. Many communications occur at informal forums and
at meetings (including phone conversations) with constituents,
lobbyists, and other legislators, none of which are covered by

the rules defining the right to know. Nor do these rules open to public view the informal forums at which compromises on legislation or trades for support of legislation are made. Often exchanges of information, advocacy by legislators, compromises, trades, and debates occur at party caucuses. These caucuses, discussed in section C1 of this chapter, are used to shape party positions on particular legislation. This is of particular significance in a two-party political system in which members of the party may share widely varying views. These meetings, when they are of the majority party of a legislative body, take on added importance and almost formal status, in the event that a caucus decision is determinative of legislative action. Most jurisdictions do not require that caucus meetings be open to public view or that records be kept of their proceedings, but in a number of jurisdictions considerable debate surrounds this practice. See generally Abner J. Mikva and Eric Lane, Legislative Process (1995).

Accessibility also includes the right of the people to petition their legislators for the redress of problems. As Justice Black has said, "the whole concept of representation depends upon the ability of the people to make their wishes known to their representatives." Eastern Railroad Presidents Conference v. Noerr Motors, 365 U.S. 127, 137 (1961). This right to petition enjoys protection against formal limitation under the U.S. Constitution (the First Amendment) and under state constitutions. But the right to petition does not require a petition to be heard. That obligation of legislators is established by the election process and the ethos of the legislative environment.

a. The Role of Organized Lobbying

Each year, legislators in all of the nation's legislative bodies receive countless communications (written and oral) from their constituents and various interest groups, urging them to advance or defeat some particular idea in the legislative arena. It is this activity that is broadly characterized as *lobbying*. These communications vary greatly in detail, from simple expressions of desire or support for new or pending legislation to detailed, factually intensive argumentation. Many of these are spontaneous and personalized communications from individual constituents. Others are the direct or indirect products of efforts by organized interests. For the most part, we will address the latter, which, for purposes of this section, are characterized as lobbying.

Organized lobbying efforts abound in every capitol in the United States. This is a by-product of representative democracy. To be effective in the legislative process people must band together and apply pressure. This is at the heart of electorally enforced representation. "[P]ractical politicians and scholars alike generally have concurred that interest groups (also known as factions, pressure groups, and special interests) are natural phenomena in a democratic regime — that is, individuals will band together to protect their interests." Allan J. Cigler and Burdett A. Loomis, Introduction, Interest Group Politics 2 (3d. ed. 1991).

In the United States, groups representing every issue imaginable form to advocate or resist the adoption of some legislation or changes to the legislative process. The Congressional Quarterly's Guide to Congress (1982) lists numerous categories of lobbying groups that include those representing business, labor, the environment, farmers, civil rights, state and local interests, foreign interests, senior citizens, education, and various single interests (for example, pro-choice movement, pro-life movement, National Rifle Association). Consumer groups and groups interested primarily in reforming the legislative process (the so-called good government groups) can also be added to this list. Groups, in a sense, breed new groups. "Groups formed from an imbalance of interests in one area induce a subsequent disequilibrium, which acts as a catalyst for individuals to form groups as counterweights to the new perceptions of inequity. Group politics thus is characterized by successive waves of mobilization and countermobilization." Allan J. Cigler and Burdett A. Loomis, Introduction, Interest Group Politics 7 (3d ed. 1991).

Lobbying is vital to the legislative process. The movement of almost all bills through legislatures is accompanied by a lobbying effort. Bills would not move without such efforts, as most frequently it is the lobbying efforts alone that create the pressure for action. Without the efforts of lobbyists, many significant problems would remain unaddressed and many resolutions to problems would be inadequate.

To influence legislative decision making, a lobbyist must first gain access to the legislative process. In the legislative arena, access means securing a legislator's attention on a particular position, on the need for specific legislation, or on the need to defeat specific legislation. Of particular importance is getting the attention of legislators who have a significant role in the process affecting the issue, such as the speaker or majority leader of the legislative body or relevant committee or subcommittee chairpersons or members. Access is an extremely important currency in the legislative process. While it does not assure a favorable outcome for the lobbyist, given the great demand for and limited supply of a legislator's time, access can provide an advantage for those who have it. This is especially true in efforts to delay, weaken, or defeat legislation, which require far less energy than passing legislation does.

To gain access, a lobbyist plays on a number of factors: the legislator's political interest in the issue, the legislator's personal interest in the issue, and the legislator's sense of obligation to the particular lobbyist or the interest represented.

The first and foremost factor, political interest, generally relates to the relationship of the subject matter to the legislator's constituency. A legislator's political interest also may relate to the legislator's ambition for higher office. The second factor, personal interest, relates to a legislator's own substantive interests — his or her own sense of "public interest." A legislator's self-image, for example, as an environmentalist or foreign policy expert, comes within this classification of interest. The final factor, sense of obligation, is a miscellaneous category relating to obligations owing from campaign contributions, requests of friends and colleagues, and similar relationships.

Access to the process includes both direct and indirect contact between the lobbyist and the legislators. Direct contact includes written communications by the lobbyist to members of the legislature, testimony before legislative committees, and meetings with legislators. An appearance before a legislative committee is the most formal method of organized lobbying. It is also the one instance of lobbying that becomes part of the official legislative history of a particular bill. Notwithstanding this, the significance of such testimony to the legislator depends on the evaluation of factors noted earlier.

Meetings with relevant legislators (those that make a difference on a particular issue) are the most favored form of direct communications but the hardest to accomplish. Most legislators do not have enough time (or interest) to meet with everyone who wishes to meet with them. Nor can legislative staff accommodate all of the demands for meetings. A prime reason why lobbyists are frequently found in public spaces (chamber lobbies or near elevators) is to create an opportunity for even casual communication with a legislator — to grab his or her ear. Whether a meeting is scheduled depends on a lobbyist's ability to appeal to a legislator's varied political, personal, or other interests.

Indirect contacts are communications to a legislator by his or her constituents that are inspired by a lobbyist or lobbying interest but are usually intended to seem as independent from him or her as possible. These communications are referred to as grass-roots campaigns. These campaigns potentially have significant effects on legislators, as they may appear (and are intended to appear) to the legislator as involving large numbers of constituents operating with intensity. Usually these communications take the form of letters or phone calls from constituents, but also include other forms of contacts such as visits by constituents with the legislator.

The proliferation of interest groups since the early years of the twentieth century has engendered a debate on their impact. The academic side of the debate offers two basic views. The first, the pluralist view, is that competition among groups assures that no single interest dominates the legislative process and produces legislative results that represent the diversity of public demands. This view is challenged by scholars who worry that a governmental system that in fact provides some success to almost all interests ("interest group liberalism") undermines the legitimacy of the legislative process because it substitutes a legislative judgment on what is the common good for compromises giving each interest group something. For a full discussion of these views, see Allan J. Cigler and Burdett A. Loomis, Introduction, Interest Group Politics 3-5 (3d ed. 1991). The question of how the common good is determined in a representative democracy is an important question. Is it simply the product of a properly working legislative process, or is there some objective standard against which to measure a statute to determine whether a statute is consistent with the common good?

The public perceives lobbying with great skepticism. They often see organized lobbying as the rapacious efforts of special interests to get their way at the cost of democracy. Sometimes this is true. Both lobbyists and legislators have been guilty of excesses in the enactment process. But, to a large extent, this view is grounded in a rhetoric of politics that casts opposition views as corrupt rather than different. Almost all nonincumbents, for example, run on a platform of "ending the grip of special interests on" whatever legislative body they are running for. Of course, if they win, their challenger uses this same issue against them.

One problem intrinsic to the growth of organized lobbying efforts is the potential these efforts have for drowning out the voices of less organized groups. There is no question that on occasion a well-organized lobbying effort for a particular issue produces a favorable result without serious legislative assessment of the costs of such victory to, for example, a less well-organized or unconcerned majority. This is an inherent problem of the legislative process, particularly in light of the need for campaign contributions. Usually such successes are restricted to narrow issues that provide perhaps large benefits to the successful interest, but only marginal increased costs to the remainder of the citizenry, for example, a particular tax break to an industry or even an individual company.

Another intrinsic problem is the potential organized efforts have for drowning out the voices of a legislator's constituents, skewing the representative relationship between representatives and their electorate. Judge Mikva recalls that when he was a state legislator in Illinois, he had proposed legislation to move state gasoline tax revenues from an earmarked fund available only for highway repairs to a general fund available for general state purposes. Suddenly Representative Mikva started receiving a considerable number (over 15 would probably qualify on an issue of this sort) of unfavorable constituent mail on his proposal. Each one was hand-addressed and hand-written and contained the same message in slightly different form. Mikva discovered that they had one similarity: All had his middle initial incorrect, an error found on the mailing list of the Illinois Automobile Association, an organization that opposed the legislation. For Representative Mikva, this discovery made a significant difference in his consideration of the legislation. Spontaneous communication from constituents would have made him extremely concerned that he had missed something with respect to the legislative proposal. On the other hand, views of an interest group that had a direct interest in the outcome of the legislation would raise far less concern. That, of course, is why the IAA lobbied in the way that it did.

b. The Regulation of Lobbying

Concerned about the consequences of large-scale lobbying efforts, Congress has enacted two major lobbying acts. The first, the Regulation of Lobbying Act of 1946, 2 U.S.C. §§261 et seq., was a hastily and poorly drafted statute that effected a broad disclosure strategy, requiring the filing of an array of information about organized lobbying efforts. Much of this statute was declared unconstitutionally vague or in violation of the First Amendment in United States v. Harriss, 347 U.S. 612 (1953). The result of this decision was a much weakened disclosure bill that among other things, excluded disclosure of organized grass-roots efforts, left ambiguous whether the lobbying of legislative staff was covered, and provided a huge loophole for organizations that claimed that lobbying was not their "principal purpose." From 1953 through 1995, numerous efforts to amend the 1946 act failed. In each instance the efforts have been vigorously opposed by groups intended to be covered, and in each case the efforts have failed. For a detailed presentation of these efforts, see Thomas M. Susman and the ABA Section of Administrative Law and Regulatory Practice, Lobbying Manual ch. 8 (1993). Finally, Congress enacted the Lobbying Disclosure Act of 1995, which extends disclosure requirements to numerous categories of lobbyists exempted from the 1946 act but does not extend coverage to grass-roots lobbying campaigns.

Laws requiring the registration of lobbyists are common among the states. For the most part, these laws follow the federal model, focusing on the registration of those who are compensated for attempting to directly influence the enactment of legislation. Many states also regulate grass-roots lobbying efforts.

C.   THE STRUCTURES OF THE LEGISLATIVE PROCESS

In the opening pages of this chapter we discussed the complexity and richness of the legislative process and the characteristics intended to legitimize it. The process occurs within a formal legislative structure compelled to some extent by the U.S. and state constitutions, by statutes, by legislative and legislative party rules. Parts of the legislative structure are noted in Professor Lane's description of New York State's legislative process (pages 60-65). While most readers are familiar with committees and their role in the legislative process, far fewer are probably familiar with the role of party leadership, conferences, and legislative staff. It is the goal of this section to introduce the major structures of the legislative process.

In basic outline, Congress and all of this nation's state legislatures are similarly structured. Each, except for Nebraska, is divided into two houses. *Bicameralism* is one of the deliberative legislative characteristics intended to make the enactment of legislation difficult. Each legislative house is organized by political party affiliations, through party caucuses or conferences, and by committees. Each house also has its own leadership structure. There is also a staff structure that includes administrative, professional, and political staffs. Within each house there also may be a number of more informal, interest-related groups, such as the Democratic Study Group of the House of Representatives, the Congressional Black Caucus, and the House Republican Freshmen (during 1995 and 1996). While these latter groups will not be part of the following exposition, at any given moment they may exercise critical power in the legislative process. For example, because of their numbers and unified commitment to certain issues, the House Republican Freshmen played a crucial role in House activities in 1995 and 1996.

1.   The Party Organization

The party system is the most significant organizational unit in Congress and many state legislatures. Legislators run for office as Democrats or Republicans and, once in the legislature, organize themselves according to these labels. In each house of Congress, and in each house of most state legislatures, each party has a caucus (often referred to as a conference) made up of all legislators of that party. The U.S. House of Representatives, for example, has the Democratic Caucus and the Republican Conference. The U.S. Senate has the Democratic and Republican Conferences. These are formal organizations that meet regularly in most jurisdictions and adopt and operate under their own caucus by-laws and customs.

The caucuses also establish committees to aid in the performance of their functions. For example, the Democratic Caucus of the U.S. House of Representatives for the 103rd Congress, 1993-1994 had the Democratic Personnel Committee (patronage), the Democratic Steering and Policy Committee (legislative scheduling and committee assignments), and the Democratic Congressional Campaign Committee (campaign support for House seats). The Republican Conference of the House had the National Republican Congressional Committee (campaign support), the Republican Committee on Committees (committee appointments), the Republican Policy Committee (legislative strategy), and the Republican Research Committee (developments of policy alternatives).

Although the legislative caucuses bear the name of national and state political parties, to a substantial extent they exist separately from these parties. National and state parties are dominated by presidential and gubernatorial politics. Power for these parties is achieved through successful executive elections. This requires making choices among the many disparate views that constitute a single party in a two-party system in order to create a platform on which to run. If the national or state party elects a chief executive, that executive usually appoints the leader of the national or state party and totally control its efforts. The executive's programs become the national or state party's programs. Power for legislative caucuses comes from having as large a membership as possible. As discussed below, the majority party dominates the legislative process, and the larger the majority the greater this domination. This creates, within the legislative caucus, a distaste for ideological choices that might drive members from its ranks.

These different approaches for gaining power cause tension between legislative caucuses (parties) and their national and state counterparts. Frequently this leads to considerable friction between a particular executive and the legislative caucuses of the executive's party. Although there are very successful efforts to create unified positions between executives and the caucuses of their party, often this unity is accomplished only through significant policy compromises by the executive. This process contrasts sharply with the process followed in most other democracies. In those countries, policy making is the purview of the prime minister and his or her cabinet, who are members of the legislature and leaders of the majority party. Legislation is adopted as introduced, party membership determines voting, and the failure to carry a measure can topple a government.

The legislative party system serves two functions: legislative governance and legislative consensus building or policy making. As an institution of governance, the party system determines legislative, committee, and subcommittee leadership; the allocation of staff and financial resources; and the daily flow of legislative activities. As a consensus builder, the caucus serves as a forum for policy and political debate, hammering out critical differences among party members on many issues in order to provide for a unified front to the opposite party on the floor of the chamber.

This unifying role is particularly important given this country's two-party system, in which legislators in one party may hold a variety of conflicting points of view. In fact, almost every view on every issue is represented in each party. Individuals choose to become Democrats or Republicans for a wide variety of reasons. Sometimes it has to do with support for particular legislative positions, but more likely these choices are determined by broader perceptions of the party's views of defining events (the Vietnam War) or perceptions (pro-labor, pro-business), or by family tradition, culture, or opportunity. Democratic and Republican legislators, may be for or against government regulation of abortion, for or against more aid to the poor, for or against higher or lower taxes, for or against more regulation of industry to protect the environment, or for or against free trade treaties. Such disparate interests and views must be melded to advance legislation.

In studying the functions of legislative caucuses, a distinction must be made between the majority and minority caucus of each house. In an institution that operates by majority vote, the majority will have more power. In a house with a strong majority (number of members as a percentage of the whole and cohesiveness), the majority caucus will control both governance of its house's process and the substance of the legislation it produces. It is a general rule of legislative practice that, in any legislative house, a majority of the majority party (although it is not a majority of the whole house) can block the consideration of legislation. This means that even if a bill is reported from a committee (and all committees have a majority of members from the majority caucus), it must gain the support of a majority of the members of the majority caucus before it can be considered or adopted by the house which that caucus controls.

The stronger (that is, the more unified and more numerous) the majority caucus is, the more reactive the minority caucus becomes. But even the weakest minority caucus has some bargaining power. The control of a legislative house depends on cooperation from the minority caucus. A determined minority caucus, through proactive use of the legislative rules and liberal use of amendments, can ensnarl the process procedurally and obstruct legislative progress substantially.

Not every bill before every caucus requires a caucus consensus in support or opposition. Sometimes the function of a caucus is simply to provide an explanatory briefing on the substance of particular bills, with no concern for reaching a caucus view. This may reflect a weak caucus (one in which it is impossible to forge a consensus), but it also may reflect a decision by the caucus that there is no reason to try to forge a consensus on the bill or that to attempt to forge a party view would be damaging to the party. For example, there may be no interest in forging a consensus over technical amendments to regulatory legislation, or there may be no possible way of forging a consensus over death penalty or abortion legislation or other issues that trigger intense personal and political responses.

Arriving at a caucus consensus does not mean that all members of the caucus will support the caucus position. Some legislators, depending on the issue, simply will not agree. There are no formal rules for dealing with such deviation. Caucuses are not ideological but pragmatic institutions that encourage as broad a membership as possible. The creation of rules about voting would work against this model. And while there is a substantial correlation between caucus membership and voting on bills over which competing caucuses are in conflict, supporting a position not followed by a majority of the members of the caucus will, most frequently, go unquestioned, particularly when the deviation from the caucus view is justified on the basis of constituent needs. But on occasion, greater premiums are placed on party loyalty. This occurs when a caucus, usually at the initiation of its leadership, decides that a particular bill is of unusual significance to its interests. The bill in effect is made a "party" bill. There is usually no formal determination of such status but its recognition flows from caucus debate. In such cases, there is greater pressure on members of the caucus to support the bill, but there is still considerable tolerance for variance from the party position, particularly if the party position is at evident odds with the interests of the dissenter's district. Such tolerance emphasizes the point made earlier about the practical, nonideological nature of legislative caucuses and the importance of constituent views to a legislator. On the other hand, consistent variance from consensus positions may make it difficult for a legislator to gain or maintain a prominent caucus role.

2. Legislative Leadership

Among the most important decisions that a legislative caucus makes is the choice of its leadership. The ability of a legislature to respond to problems perceived as needing legislative response depends on the existence of some formal leadership to administer the legislative process and meld disparate views toward a solution that will be acceptable to a majority of the legislators.

Leadership structures in Congress and in most state legislatures are similar. The most populous house (usually known as the house of representatives or assembly) has a speaker (constitutionally required), and the least populous house (the senate) has a president. In the U.S. Senate and in the senates of many state legislatures, the vice president and lieutenant governors serve as presidents of the Senate. Usually, they have very limited powers: to preside over the body and to cast votes in case of a tie. In these bodies, legislative leadership is usually provided by the majority leader, as in the U.S. Senate, or by a temporary president (president pro tem). In some states, lieutenant governors play a more active role in the process, for example, participating in committee assignments and scheduling the consideration of legislation. Finally, in some states there is no lieutenant governor, or the lieutenant governor is assigned no legislative tasks at all. See generally Alan Rosenthal, Legislative Life 150 (1981). Speakers and temporary presidents are the only members of the legislative leadership chosen by their respective houses. All other positions are chosen by legislative caucuses. They include, with some variation from legislature to legislature, a majority leader, assistant majority leaders, a minority leader, assistant minority leaders, majority and minority whips, and majority and minority assistant whips. (Whips and assistant whips are appointed by each party caucus to aid the legislative leaders in implementing the party's legislative strategy. Their primary function is communicating with members and overseeing floor activity.)

The tasks of legislative leadership are multitudinous. The following description about congressional leadership applies to both state and local legislatures. "Leaders help to organize orderly consideration of legislative proposals, promote party support for or against legislation, attempt to reconcile differences that threaten to disrupt the chambers, plan strategy on important legislation, consult with the [executive], and publicize legislative achievements." Walter J. Oleszek, Congressional Procedures and the Policy Process 28 (1989). They also are the focal point for asserting legislative prerogative against incursions from either the executive or legislative branch of government.

To effect these tasks, legislative leaders are granted various powers by legislative rules and tradition. Among these are, the choice of committee chairs, appointments to committees, scheduling of legislation, and the referrals of bills to particular committees. The distribution of these powers among the legislative leadership, party caucuses, and committee chairs has shifted, historically, as reformers have responded to excesses of either centralized or decentralized power. For example, after the 1994 elections in which the Republicans took control of the House of Representatives, Speaker Newt Gingrich raced to assert centralized leadership over his party caucus and the House before the newly elected chairs of the various committees could establish themselves and begin pulling against the legislative platform (the Contract with America) advocated by the Speaker and his leadership circle.

Legislative leadership is not self-ordained. As a rule, successful legislative leaders are continuously alert to the fact that their power is "derived from the coherence of the party membership and the degree to which the members of each party identify their own legislative priorities with the agenda set by the party leadership. Otherwise . . . the leader is a general without soldiers." Abner J. Mikva and Patti B. Saris, The American Congress 86 (1983).

3. Legislative Committees

Standing committees are the locus of most legislative activity. Standing committees are the permanent committees that have the authority to consider and report bills and conduct oversight investigations. To understand the legislative process, one has to understand the functions and procedures of legislative committees. All bills are assigned to committees, and most never leave them. It is the committee, for the most part, that decides whether a particular problem raised by a bill merits formal legislative attention and whether the solution posed by the bill is appropriate for formal legislative consideration. These decisions are usually discretionary. A committee may simply ignore a bill by failing to consider it. Or, a committee may substantially rewrite a bill so that the amended version provides an entirely different solution than did the original one. "Committees decide with respect to legislation what will be buried, what will barely come out of committee, and what will come out with a favored likelihood of enactment." Charles Tiefer, Congressional Practice and Procedure 57-58 (1989).

One of the most significant decisions a committee or subcommittee makes is whether to hold a hearing. This decision, in most cases, determines a committee's policy priorities and commits a considerable amount of its resources. "At both the full and subcommittee level, hearings are seldom a paragon of spontaneity. They are carefully mapped out and scripted in advance." Abner J. Mikva and Patti B. Saris, The American Congress 210 (1983). There are two types of hearings: legislative and oversight. "In a legislative hearing, the focus is on a particular bill or bills. . . . In an oversight hearing, the focus is on the functioning of some federal program or agency — its efficiency, obedience to statutory mandate, or new policies — or some private sector problem." Charles Tiefer, Congressional Practice and Procedure 149 (1989).

The overall function of a legislative hearing is to create a public record on which to base legislative activity. There is no legal requirement for such a public record, nor even for holding a hearing on a bill. Members gain information about problems and proposed solutions from numerous sources and in many different ways, with hearings being only one such source. Indeed, this is one of the reasons that many committee hearings, particularly legislative hearings, are poorly attended by legislative members. But hearings can be enormously important beyond their value of informing legislators about a proposed bill. First, they focus public attention on a particular subject. Second, they serve as a public record for why a legislature acted in a particular fashion. This record may have implications for subsequent administrative and judicial action. Third, they provide a forum at which the public can evaluate the significance of the subject under review. Fourth, they establish a forum at which legislators can be evaluated. And finally, they provide a formal opportunity for interested parties to be heard on a particular bill.

Most witnesses at hearings are not the "average citizen" but are representatives of the executive branch (particularly for oversight hearings) and of various organizations and associations who are interested in the proposed legislation. In most instances, witnesses are eager or at least willing to appear before committee. But on occasion, people are unwilling to testify or produce the documents requested. In these instances, the committee may issue a subpoena to require such testimony or documents. All legislative bodies have the power to issue subpoenas for legislative purposes, although different legislative institutions may have different rules on issuance procedures.

After a hearing on a bill has been completed, a committee must next decide whether to act on the proposal. If a committee decides to act, the bill enters into its markup phase. It is during the markup period that a bill receives its most concentrated institutional study. The bill becomes the "mark." It is read line-by-line to the members of the committee, usually in an open session of the committee. During this period, explanations for particular provisions are offered, discussions go on, and amendments are offered and considered.

The number of standing committees and subcommittees, their jurisdiction, and size of their membership and party ratio (number of majority party and minority party members as a percentage of the total number of members) is usually established by the rules of each chamber, although in the U.S. House of Representatives, for example, the number of members for each committee and party ratio is determined by the Speaker in consultation with the minority leader. The number of members on a committee is the product of a number of factors, most significantly the demand for seats on particular committees by members of the majority caucus. In most cases, the party ratio relates to percentage of members each party has in the particular chamber, although this may vary.

Appointments to committee are generally recommended by caucus committees (for example, the Policy and Steering Committee of the Democratic Caucus of the House of Representatives), in consultation with legislative leadership, and approved by each respective caucus. In most legislative bodies, such as Congress, they are then "elected" by their respective houses. In both houses of Congress and in most state legislatures there is an unwritten "property right" rule that reelected members can maintain (with seniority) the committee assignments they had in the previous legislative term, unless they ask for a transfer. The significance of committees to legislative work creates considerable competition for open seats. Members see committees as a way to help their constituents, further their reelection goals, join the party leadership, and further their policy agendas. The assignment to an open committee seat is determined by a number of factors, including seniority, caucus loyalty, leadership loyalty, political needs, and geography. The choice of committee chairs and of ranking minority members are also subject to the approval of the respective legislative caucuses.

Congress, unlike state legislatures, has an extensive subcommittee system that has been spawned over the last half of the twentieth century. Subcommittees in Congress are the product of a number of factors, including workloads that involve greater concentrations of expertise and focus, the ambition of more members for more involvement in the legislative action, and a desire on the part of some members, historically, to circumvent the power of certain committee chairs. Most often, the number of subcommittees, their jurisdiction, their size, party ratio, and membership are determined by the members of the parent committee, acting through committed political caucuses. The expansion of the subcommittee system, particularly in the U.S. House, has been the subject of considerable criticism. The thrust of this criticism is that the establishment of subcommittees on the congressional scale seriously decentralizes power, making the enactment of legislation more difficult than it would be without the subcommittees. For these critics, each subcommittee becomes an additional obstacle that a bill must overcome in order to be enacted into law.

Legislative reliance on committees raises issues about the representative nature of legislative committees. Committees are almost always unrepresentative, to varying degrees, of the parent chamber. No committee is an exact reflection of the interest mix of its parent body, and many are quite different. Professor Fenno, in his study of congressional committees, shows that the Interior Committee of the House, during his period of study, had a pro-development, Western bias that was inconsistent with the more conservationist view of the House itself. Richard D. Fenno, Jr., Congressmen in Committees (1973). Such imbalances reflect, to a large extent, the relationship between the jurisdiction of the committees and goals of individual legislators. For example, during the period of Fenno's study, the jurisdiction of the Interior Committee included projects affecting irrigation, mines, national parks, and the like. Each of the members on this committee believed that service to their constituents was their primary legislative goal. Such service would be performed by advancing projects favored by their constituents, who were most frequently in favor of the development of land resources. It would have been far less likely that representatives who opposed such projects would have joined this committee. Their experience on the committee would have been extremely negative (voting no on projects) and would have been hard to translate into a meaningful reelection theme. Most representatives would prefer to battle such projects on the floor of the legislative chamber, reserving committee time for more affirmative efforts.

The unrepresentativeness of legislative committees is far less of a concern when committees report legislation than when they kill it. The reporting of legislation means that it can be subject to the will of the chamber; the killing of legislation usually means that it will not be considered by the chamber. In killing legislation, committees, if they are particularly unrepresentative, may be frustrating the representative interests of the remainder of the parent chamber. This last point is somewhat ironic. Created to make the legislative process more efficient, committees can also make the legislative process less representative by allowing a committee chair or unrepresentative membership to kill a bill. This singular power of a committee to kill legislation has led to the development of a number of practices and rules for circumventing committee power.

The rules of most legislative bodies provide for some method of discharging a bill from a committee without that committee's support. These discharge procedures are, in theory, escape valves for the pressure created by popularly supported legislation that is being bottled up in a committee. For an example of the procedure that must be followed in making a motion to discharge, see Rule XXVII (4) of the Rules of the House of Representatives. There are considerable pressures against the use of motions to discharge (as there are against other efforts to undermine committee authority). Supporters of such motions, in fact, are second-guessing the decisions of their colleagues on the committee and may be similarly second-guessed in the future. For this reason, motions to discharge rarely succeed.

Sometimes legislative bodies undertake unique efforts to assure full consideration of a bill. For example, in Chapter Three, pages 109 to 111, Senator Mansfield's motion to require the Senate Judiciary Committee to report the Voting Rights Act of 1965 by a certain date is a procedure intended to deny the hostile Judiciary Committee the power to kill the bill. The hostility of that Judiciary Committee was a result of a then-controlling seniority system that allowed long-tenured southern democratic senators to gain a unique grip on the Senate through the control of many important committees, despite the minority status of southern senators as a whole.

4. Legislative Staff

Many thousands of people work for legislative bodies. Basically they fall into several categories: administrative, clerical, political (the personal staffs of legislators), and policy (committee staff and staff of such support organizations as the Congressional Research Service). In Congress and most state legislatures, the growth of staff has accompanied the growth of legislative activities discussed in Chapter One. The staff of Congress dwarfs that of any state legislature, but among state legislatures the number of staff members vary. See generally Alan Rosenthal, Legislative Life (1981).

Of particular significance is the role that policy staff members play in the lawmaking process. In Congress, for example, there are over three thousand committee staff members. Clearly they have an impact on the process and its substance. For the most part the role of staff is constructive. Without staff, neither Congress nor any legislative body would be able to maintain a central policy or oversight roll, particularly when matched against a well-staffed executive. Furthermore, staff members free legislators to focus on and resolve major controversies, ones that staff members are not able to forge a consensus on themselves.

The staff may have considerable leverage over marginal issues, but it does not extend to the major concerns of constituents. The

arm twisting and peer-group pressure necessary to enact any
piece of controversial legislation remains the prerogative of the
members. . . . Consequently, leaving the details of legislation to
the staff is not harmful but rational, sane, and effective, for then
the members are free to "wheel and deal" on the big issues.

Abner J. Mikva and Patti B. Saris, The American Congress 190
(1983).

Leaving the legislative details to staff is not without its
problems. Such details, for example, include the drafting of
committee reports, which often are unread by committee
members but become critical pieces of legislative history.
Sometimes staff members accomplish policy goals in negotia-
tions without the legislators' awareness. Legislators may vote
on amendments to a bill solely on the basis of a quick staff
briefing. The power of staff in all of these settings, of course, is
dependent on the management style of different legislators.
Some representatives give their staff wide policy authority,
while others control their actions tightly.

An interesting example of an attempt to use a staff
product in a judicial setting is provided by Giuliani v. Hevesi,
1997 N.Y. LEXIS 300, an action by the mayor of New York City
against its comptroller. An issue in the case was meaning of
the word "transfer," as found in a particular statute. To support its view of the word's meaning, the mayor's counsel, at
the trial level, submitted a contemporaneous memorandum
from a staff member of the New York State Senate minority
party as evidence "transfer" was to be read consistent with the
mayor's view. In our view, a memorandum of a minority party
staff member that was without any evidence that legislators
were aware of it should come very low, if anywhere, in any
pecking order. The court did not deal with the issue.

D. LEGISLATIVE RULES AND THEIR
     ENFORCEMENT

In the preceding parts of this chapter, we discussed the
dynamics, characteristics, and structures of the legislative
process. In every house of every legislature and most legisla-

tive caucuses and committees, this process operates under a set of procedural rules. These rules govern everything from the form of a bill, to the method of its introduction, to the manner by which a bill is considered at every step in the legislative process, to the votes necessary to enact legislation. Rules bring procedural order to the legislative process and offer protection to minority interests. They "determine the ways in which collective decisions are made, and they constitute the context in which individual members pursue their policy and political objectives and attempt to maximize their legislative achievement." Stanley Bach, The Nature of Congressional Rules, 5 J.L. & Politics 725, 726 (1989). Examples of legislative rules operating in the enactment process are found in Chapter Three.

Some of these rules are found in the federal and state constitutions. Of these constitutions, the U.S. Constitution contains the fewest requirements for processing bills. Article I, §5 designates a majority of each house of Congress as a quorum for doing business, mandates a journal, and provides for recorded votes in certain circumstances. Article I, §7 contains the veto process. State constitutions are filled with considerably more procedural detail.

Most legislative procedural rules are part of the standing rules of legislative bodies. These are enacted under grants of power found in the federal and all state constitutions. These grants are all similar to Article I, §5 of the U.S. Constitution, which provides: "Each House may determine the Rules of its Proceedings." The rules of a particular house are usually published and available. The rules of the House of Representatives are found in a document known as the Constitution, Jefferson's Manual, and the Rules of the House of Representatives, and the rules of the Senate are found in a document known as Senate Manual Containing the Standing Rules, Orders, Laws, and Resolutions Affecting the Business of the United States Senate. They are available from the Government Printing Office. Committee and caucus rules, if written, are less accessible and must be requested from the particular caucus or committee. Regarding the House of Representatives, the term rule can sometimes be confusing. In the House, almost every bill that is reported to the legislative floor is accompanied by its own "rule," adopted by the Rules Committee and the House for the purpose of governing debate on that particular bill. These individual rules are not part of the standing rules of the House, although the rule that there be a unique governing rule for each bill is.

Legislative rules serve a variety of functions. The key ones among them, according to the political scientist Walter J. Oleszek," are to provide stability, legitimize decisions, divide responsibilities, reduce conflict and distribute power." Walter J. Oleszek, Congressional Procedures and the Policy Process 5 (1989). Additionally, legislative rules provide opportunities for members of the minority caucus or individual legislators to protect themselves against legislative excesses by majorities.

Legislative rules do not simply frame process. They shape policy. The skillful use of rules may preclude consideration of some issues and expedite consideration of others. The use of rules in this fashion often fosters policy compromises. For example, the threat or use of a filibuster (see Chapter Three, section C8) may result in policy compromises to move legislation forward.

For the most part, legislative bodies enforce their own rules. If rules become too restraining in a particular situation, most legislative bodies "are free to set aside most rules, or create temporary rules, by unanimous consent, and they do so daily. . . . Whatever procedures are being followed by the House or Senate, whatever legislative rules are in effect, its members retain the power to enforce them or not, as they choose." Stanley Bach, The Nature of Congressional Rules, 5 J.L. & Politics 725, 737-739 (1989). Sometimes, however, disputes over legislative rules reach the courts. At the federal level, these cases are almost always unsuccessful because of the absence of any significant procedural details in the U.S. Constitution and the constitutional authority that each legislative house may determine its own rules. See, for example, United States v. Ballin, 144 U.S. 1 (1891) (a challenge on the meaning of the term quorum), and Vander Jagt v. O'Neill, 699 F.2d 1166 (D.C. Cir. 1983) (a challenge to the ratio of Democrats to Republicans on certain committees of the House of Representatives).

State courts, because of the inclusion of procedural details in state constitutions, have been far more active as forums for determining the validity of legislative procedures. See generally Robert F. Williams, State Constitutional Limits on Legislative Procedure: Legislative Compliance and Judicial Enforcement, 48 U. Pitt. L. Rev. 797 (1987). Professor Williams has written:

> State courts have developed a surprisingly wide range of approaches to enforcing restriction on legislative procedure under circumstances where an act does not violate procedural limitations on its face. Even within single jurisdictions, one can detect inconsistent doctrines and a lack of continuity over time. These widely varying judicial doctrines reflect what are essentially political decisions, made in the context of adjudicating actual controversies, concerning the extent of judicial enforcement of state constitutional norms.

Id. at 816.

Two New York decisions illustrate the type of range that Professor Williams refers to. In King v. Cuomo, 613 N.E.2d 950 (N.Y. 1993), the issue before the court was the validity of a legislative rule that permitted the recall of a bill from the governor after it had been formally presented to the governor pursuant to the state constitution's presentment clause. The goal of the recall procedure was to avoid vetoes that would have imposed political costs on either the bill's sponsor or the governor. Sometimes the governor would warn the legislator of a pending veto and accept a recall. Sometimes the governor would ask for a recall to avoid using the veto power. The court invalidated this practice, despite a constitutional provision authorizing the legislature to determine its own rules of procedure, based on its view that once presented to governor, the bill was outside the legislature's domain.

Heimbach v. New York, 453 N.E.2d 1264 (N.Y. 1982), presents the other side of the *King* rule. In this case, the question was a legislative voting method that in certain cases authorized votes to be attributed to legislators, although they were not present in the legislative chamber when the vote was cast. A member of the state senate had been registered as a "yes" vote on several taxes (which, in the case, he stated that he opposed) during a period of day in which he had been in the hospital. The affirmative votes were registered because of a state senate rule that, on certain types of roll calls, counted every member who had checked in as a "yes" vote, if that member was not on the floor to vote "no." In this case, the

New York Court of Appeals upheld the legislative procedure, based on its view that the dispute was an internal legislative dispute and conclusively subject to the legislature's rules.

CHAPTER THREE _____

The Enactment of a Statute

In Chapter Two we broadly describe the legislative process, explore the features that provide its legitimacy, and focus on the structures and rules through which the process proceeds. In this chapter we address the actual enactment process, following the passage of a particular bill through each house of Congress to the president's desk. Both the interpretation of statutes and the practice of legislative law require familiarity with the steps and language of the legislative process, and such familiarity is the goal of this chapter.

A. THE VOTING RIGHTS ACT OF 1965

The Voting Rights Act of 1965 was one of the most significant pieces of legislation ever adopted by Congress. Its passage, the result of an intense grass-roots campaign by the civil rights movement, placed the federal government squarely behind efforts to create equal opportunities for African Americans to participate in the political process. As the 89th Congress organized itself in January 1965, passage of a broad voting rights reform was not a certainty. Although the newly elected president, Lyndon B. Johnson, was committed to such reform and Congress was controlled by Democrats, many of the Democrats (along with many Republicans) opposed significant federal involvement in securing voting rights. Because of the then dominant seniority rules, many of these members held significant positions in Congress and could be counted on to take every opportunity to obstruct serious voting rights legislation.

In the presentation that follows, we will watch the 89th Congress (1965-1966) consider the voting rights bills that became the Voting Rights Act of 1965. Our window will be the Congressional Record, in which much of the formal work of Congress is recorded.

B.   RECORDING LEGISLATIVE ACTIVITIES — THE CONGRESSIONAL RECORD

Since 1873, the Congressional Record has published daily the proceedings and debates of the U.S. Congress. The Congressional Record is bound annually with an Index and Daily Digest. While the journal of each house (a constitutionally mandated document distinct from the Congressional Record) serves as the official record of legislative votes, the Congressional Record serves as an authoritative record of the proceedings of Congress. Each day, the Congressional Record includes, a list of all bills introduced by legislators or reported from any committee in each legislative house, the full text of bills considered on the legislative floor and the text of any amendments to those bills, the text of any conference committee reports and amendments taken up on the legislative floor, and a full record of legislative debate and remarks.

Users of the Congressional Record must be careful. Although a statute requires the Congressional Record to "be substantially a verbatim report of proceedings" 44 U.S.C. §901, historically, congressional rules have allowed members of Congress to make some poststatement editing of remarks and, under certain conditions, to insert into the Congressional Record remarks not made on the legislative floor. The poststatement editing has been the subject of considerable criticism because it permitted members, after asking for permission from their particular house "to revise and extend their remarks" (sometimes even when they have made none), to add or remove portions of a speech without any indication in the Congressional Record that the remarks recorded had not been made on the legislative floor. From interpretive perspective, this allows a legislator to create a "legislative history" without opportunity for challenge (in which case the legislator's remarks should be disregarded) or any indication that his or her remarks have not been made in legislative debate. This "corruption" of the legislative record was challenged in Gregg v. Barrett, 771 F.2d 539 (D.C. Cir. 1985), a case in which Judge Mikva, writing for the court, decided that the issue was not justiciable. In 1995, the House of Representatives, in theory, limited such uses of the Congressional Record to "technical, grammatical and typographical corrections." Rule XIV(9)(a), Rules of the House of Representatives, 104th Cong., 1st Sess. (1995).

Sometimes legislators' comments appear in the Congressional Record designated by a bullet or different typeface or under the heading "Extension of Remarks." Usually this means that no part of these comments has been delivered on the legislative floor. These "extended" remarks save floor time that might otherwise be used for their reading. For a more detailed discussion of the Congressional Record, see Congressional Quarterly, Guide to Congress, 442 (4th ed. 1991).

What the Congressional Record does not contain is any work of the congressional committees, that is, transcripts of hearings or debates or markup sessions (the committee session at which a bill is read line by line for amendment and vote) or the committees' reports.

This presentation does not include every amendment proposed, nor does it set forth, for the most part, debate on the substance of the legislation. Rather it is intended to introduce the formal mechanics and language of the legislative process and the methods for following it.

C.   THE ENACTMENT PROCESS

1.   *The Introduction of Bills*

A bill is a proposal for a change in the law that becomes a statute after it has been enacted. The bills that ultimately led to the adoption of Public Law No. 89-110, the Voting Rights Act of 1965, were introduced into the 89th Congress, First Session, on March 17, 1965, in the House of Representatives (H.R. 6400) and on March 18, 1965, in the Senate (S. 1564).

In Congress, as in most legislative bodies, ideas for legislation are introduced in the form of a bill. Ideas for legislation can emanate from a variety of sources, for example, legislators, lobbyists, constituents, legislative staffs, and, perhaps most importantly, the executive branch. For a discussion of the role of the executive branch in the initiation of legislation, see Chapter Two, section A3.

Only members of a legislature can introduce bills. However, the budget processes in some states require the governor of that state to submit budget bills to the legislature. See, for example, Cal. Const. art. IV, §12; Ill. Const. art. VIII, §2; N.Y. Const. art. VII, §2. A member who introduces a bill is known as the bill's sponsor. A bill may have a number of sponsors or cosponsors. For example S. 1564, set forth below, had 66 sponsors, enough to stop a filibuster and pass the bill. Part of the strategy of any lobbying campaign is the choice of a bill's sponsor. A bill sponsored, for example, by a new member of the minority party would have little chance of passage or consideration. On the other hand, a bill sponsored by a senior member of the majority party or by a number of members of the majority party (see S. 1564) would be taken more seriously. Similarly, a bill sponsored, as in the case of the Voting Rights Act of 1965, by the chair of the house committee to which it is assigned (Representative Celler, Judiciary) or by the Senate majority leader (Senator Mansfield) indicates serious legislative consideration. Sometimes sponsorships are deceptive. The fact of sponsorship does not always guarantee an enactment effort by the sponsor. For example, sometimes executive branch bills or constituent bills are introduced as a courtesy without clear support or with support but without a promise to push their consideration. Frequently this is indicated by a parenthetical phrase (by request) next to the name of the sponsor.

In the U.S. House of Representatives, bills are introduced by depositing a bill in the "hopper," provided for that purpose in the chamber. In the Senate, bills are usually introduced in a similar manner. On occasion, if a senator seeks some particular procedural treatment for a bill, the senator rises and introduces the bill from the floor. The latter path was followed for the in troduction of S. 1564 to assure that a hostile committee would not delay or kill the bill. In state legislative bodies, bills are usually introduced by depositing them with the clerk of the sponsor's legislative house. After introduction, bills are assigned numbers (usually sequentially) by clerks of the legislative bodies and referred to the appropriate committees by the presiding officer of each house. After a bill is introduced, in most legislative bodies, it is printed.

Only a small percentage of bills become law. The system, politically and administratively, winnows the number of bills enacted to a minimal percentage of those introduced. Bills occupy a number of cubbyholes that roughly bespeak their possibilities for passage: bills with little support, noncontroversial bills, controversial bills, major bills, and "must" bills. Bills with little support, the most frequently introduced bills, are not introduced with an enactment expectation, at least, not on the part of the legislator. They are intended generally to publicize an issue, initiate debate on such issue, or curry political favor with a constituent or interest group. The introduction of a bill can shift political "heat" from the legislator to a legislative committee. Noncontroversial bills, are bills that are expedited through the process without opposition, generally by the use of special calendars. They include bills to exchange real property, to rename parks or streets, or to name a building after a former legislator. Controversial bills are those around which swirls political controversy. They are usually major bills, those pieces of legislation that have broad redistributive or regulatory impact. The likelihood of their enactment is unpredictable. Legislative bodies focus most of their attention on these types of bills. "Must" bills are controversial bills that the legislature generally agrees must be resolved before the end of a legislative session. These bills generally garner the most attention as members struggle to find compromises to build majorities. The Voting Rights Act is an example of major, controversial, "must" legislation.

Excerpts from H.R. 6400 and S. 1564 follow. Their form is similar to the form of bills used in the nation's state legislatures.

89TH CONGRESS
1st SESSION

H.R. 6400

IN THE HOUSE OF REPRESENTATIVES

March 17, 1965

Mr. CELLER introduced the following bill; which was referred to the Committee on the Judiciary

---

A BILL

To enforce the fifteenth amendment to the Constitution of the United States.

Be it enacted by the Senate and House of Representatives of the United States of America in Congress assembled, That this Act shall be known as the "Voting Rights Act of 1965."

SEC. 2. No voting qualification or procedure shall be imposed or applied to deny or abridge the right to vote on account of race or color. . . .

89TH CONGRESS
1st SESSION

S. 1564

IN THE SENATE OF THE UNITED STATES

MARCH 18, 1965

Mr. Mansfield (for himself, Mr. Dirksen, Mr. Kuchel, Mr. Aikin, Mr. Allott, Mr. Anderson, Mr. Bartlett, Mr. Bass, Mr. Bath, Mr. Bennett, Mr. Boggs, Mr. Brewster, Mr. Burdick, Mr. Case, Mr. Church, Mr. Clark, Mr. Cooper, Mr. Cotton, Mr. Dodd, Mr. Dominick, Mr. Douglas, Mr. Fong, Mr. Gruening, Mr. Harris, Mr. Hart, Mr. Hartke, Mr. Inouye, Mr. Jackson, Mr. Javits, Mr. Jordan of Idaho, Mr. Kennedy of Massachusetts, Mr. Kennedy of New York, Mr. Lausche, Mr. Long of Missouri, Mr. Magnuson, Mr. McCarthy, Mr. McGee, Mr. McGovern, Mr. McIntyre, Mr. McNamara, Mr. Metcalf, Mr. Mondale, Mr. Monroney, Mr. Montoya, Mr. Morse, Mr. Morton, Mr. Moss, Mr. Mundt, Mr. Murphy, Mr. Muskie, Mr. Nelson, Mrs. Neuberger, Mr. Pastore, Mr. Pearson, Mr. Pell, Mr. Prouty, Mr. Proxmire, Mr. Randolph, Mr. Ribicoff, Mr. Saltonstall, Mr. Scott, Mr. Symington, Mr. Tydings, Mr. Williams of New Jersey, Mr. Yarborough, and Mr. Young of Ohio) introduced the following bill; which was read twice and referred to the Committee on the Judiciary

---

A BILL

To enforce the fifteenth amendment to the Constitution of the United States.

Be it enacted by the Senate and House of Representatives of the United States of America in Congress assembled, That this Act shall be known as the "Voting Rights Act of 1965."

SEC. 2. No voting qualification or procedure shall be imposed or applied to deny or abridge the right to vote on account of race or color.

2.   *The Assignment of Bills to Committees*

One of the most important decisions about a bill is the choice of committee to which it is assigned. (Committees' functions and structures are discussed in Chapter Two, section C3.) Committee decisions to kill bills are rarely overturned, and committee amendments usually frame the ensuing legislative debate. References to committees are usually routine acts by legislative staff under the formal authority of the legislative leadership of the particular house in which the bill has been introduced. For example, in the Congress, it is the parliamentarians who usually make the referrals. Most referrals are simple, based on the subject of the bill and the jurisdiction of the particular committee. But, while each legislative committee has its own jurisdiction (either codified or set forth in the legislative rules of the particular house), there are many jurisdictional ambiguities. The present rules of the House of Representatives provide for multiple referrals of bills whose subject matter comes within the jurisdiction of more than one committee.

The decision about which committee to refer a bill to can be of life or death significance, and the selection of a committee may be part of the overall strategy for the passage of a bill. For example, the Civil Rights Act of 1964 was drafted to permit its referral to a friendly Senate Commerce Committee rather than to a hostile Senate Judiciary Committee. But in all referrals there must be some relationship between the bill's subject matter and the committee's jurisdiction.

When the Voting Rights Act of 1965 was introduced in the Senate, it was accompanied by a motion that the Senate Judiciary Committee report the bill within a specific number of days. Typically, no formal limits circumscribe a committee's consideration of a bill. Senator Mansfield's motion, which led to the debate, was atypical and intended to ensure that the committee process did not tie up the legislation. This concern was particularly justified by proponents of the bill because the chair of the Judiciary Committee, Senator Eastland, was opposed to the legislation, and it was feared that he would exercise whatever prerogatives available to delay its movement. The motion triggered a procedural dispute that signaled the rugged debate the passage of this bill would entail.

Mr. MANSFIELD.   Mr. President, on behalf of the distinguished minority leader and myself, I move that the bill be referred
to the Committee on the Judiciary, with instructions to report back
not later than April 9, 1965.

The VICE PRESIDENT.   The question is on agreeing to the motion of the Senator from Montana.

Mr. EASTLAND.   Mr. President — .

The VICE PRESIDENT.   The motion is debatable.

The Senator from Mississippi [Mr. Eastland] is recognized.

Mr. EASTLAND.   Mr. President, as I understand, the motion is
to refer the bill to the Judiciary Committee, the bill to be reported
back not later than the 9th day of April.

The VICE PRESIDENT.   That is the understanding of the
Chair.

Mr. EASTLAND.   Mr. President, this is a bill which flies directly in the face of the Constitution of the United States. What is being
proposed is an unheard of thing. It is proposed to give the Judiciary
Committee only 15 days to study a bill as far reaching as this. Of
course, there cannot be the attention paid to it which it should have.
I assure the Senate that the Committee on the Judiciary will hold
hearings expeditiously and will go into all phases of the bill.

Let me make myself clear: I am opposed to every word and
every line in the bill. . . .

The PRESIDING OFFICER. The question is on agreeing to the
motion to refer the bill to the Committee on the Judiciary with instructions.

On this question, the yeas and nays have been ordered; and the
clerk will call the roll.

The legislative clerk proceeded to call the roll.

Mr. MANSFIELD (when his name was called).   On this vote I
have a pair with the junior Senator from Alabama [Mr. Sparkman]. If
he were present and voting he would vote "nay." If I were at liberty
to vote, I would vote "yes." I therefore withhold my vote.

Mr. METCALF (when his name was called).   On this vote I
have a pair with the senior Senator from Louisiana [Mr. Ellender]. If
he were present and voting he would vote "nay." If I were at liberty
to vote, I would vote "yea." I therefore withhold my vote.

The rollcall was concluded.

Mr. LONG of Louisiana.   I announce that the Senator from
Idaho [Mr. Church], the Senator from Louisiana [Mr. Ellender], The
Senator from Alaska [Mr. Gruening], the Senator from Missouri [Mr.
Long], the Senator from Minnesota [Mr. McCarthy], the Senator
from Oklahoma [Mr. Monroney], and the Senator from Florida [Mr.
Smathers] are absent on official business.

I also announce that the Senator from North Carolina [Mr. Ervin], the Senator from New York [Mr. Kennedy], the Senator from Wyoming [Mr. McGee], the Senator from Utah [Mr. Moss], the Senator from Georgia [Mr. Russell], and the Senator from Alabama [Mr. Sparkman] are necessarily absent.

On this vote, the Senator from New York [Mr. Kennedy] is paired with the Senator from North Carolina [Mr. Ervin]. If present and voting, the Senator from New York would vote "yea," and the Senator from North Carolina would vote "nay."

I further announce that, if present and voting, the Senator from Idaho [Mr. Church], the Senator from Missouri [Mr. Long], the Senator from Utah [Mr. Moss], the Senator from Oklahoma [Mr. Monroney], and the Senator from Alaska [Mr. Gruening] would each vote "yea."

Mr. KUCHEL.   I announce that the Senator from Utah [Mr. Bennett], the Senator from Arizona [Mr. Fannin], the Senator from California [Mr. Murphy], and the Senator from Texas [Mr. Tower] are necessarily absent.

The Senator from Massachusetts [Mr. Saltonstall] is absent on official business.

If present and voting, the Senator from Utah [Mr. Bennett], the Senator from Massachusetts [Mr. Saltonstall], the Senator from Texas [Mr. Tower], and the Senator from California [Mr. Murphy] would each vote "yea."

The result was announced — yeas 67, nays 13, as follows:

[No. 40 Leg.]

YEAS — 67

Aiken	Cooper	Hruska
Allott	Cotton	Inouye
Anderson	Curtis	Jackson
Bartlett	Dirksen	Javits
Bass	Dodd	Jordan, ID
Bayh	Dominick	Kennedy, MA
Bible	Douglas	Kuchel
Boggs	Fong	Lausche
Brewster	Fulbright	Magnuson
Burdick	Gore	McGovern
Byrd, WV	Harris	McIntyre
Cannon	Hart	McNamara
Carlson	Hartke	Miller
Case	Hayden	Mondale
Clark	Hickenlooper	Montoya

Morse   Pell   Tydings
Morton   Prouty   Williams, DE
Mundt   Proxmire   Williams, NJ
Muskie   Randolph   Yarborough
Nelson   Ribicoff   Young, ND
Neuberger   Scott   Young, OH
Pastore   Simpson
Pearson   Symington

NAYS – 13

Byrd, VA   Jordan, NC   Stennis
Eastland   Long, LA   Talmadge
Hill   McClellan   Thurmond
Holland   Robertson
Johnston   Smith

NOT VOTING – 20

Bennett   Long, MO   Murphy
Church   Mansfield   Russell
Ellender   McCarthy   Saltonstall
Ervin   McGee   Smathers
Fannin   Metcalf   Sparkman
Gruening   Monroney   Tower
Kennedy, NY   Moss

So the motion of Mr. Mansfield and other Senators to refer the bill (S. 1564) to the Committee on the Judiciary with instructions was agreed to.

Mr. JAVITS.   Mr. President, I move that the Senate reconsider the vote by which the motion was agreed to.

Mr. KUCHEL.   I move to lay that motion on the table.

The VICE PRESIDENT.   The question is on agreeing to the motion of the Senator from California to lay on the table the motion of the Senator from New York to reconsider.

The motion to lay on the table was agreed to.

3.   *Legislative Voting*

For an initial observer of the legislative process, legislative voting often seems confusing and sometimes unsettling. In addition to archaic terminology ("ayes and nays"), depending on the legislative jurisdiction one is viewing, bills can pass with few legislators on the floor, and absent legislators can be counted as voting in favor of the legislation.

Basically there are two general voting methods: nonrecorded votes, in which individual votes are not recorded (mostly limited to Congress), and recorded votes, in which individual votes are noted.

Nonrecorded votes are divided into three forms: voice votes, division votes, and teller votes. On a voice vote, votes are cast in chorus by answering "aye" or "no" to a particular question; the presiding officer determines the outcome of the vote based on the volume of the response. A division vote, which may be demanded by any member, is a more accurate form of voice vote because it requires members to stand to be counted rather than to just express their view by voice. Even more accurate is the teller vote, in which members are assigned the responsibility of making an actual count. This vote must be required by one-fifth of a quorum. Individual votes are not recorded in any of these forms. The voice vote occasionally results in legislation passing with no member on the legislature floor except for the presiding officer. Such a result can be avoided by a call for a quorum by any member. While nonrecorded votes, particularly voice votes, may afford some legislative efficiency in consideration of noncontroversial legislation, it can also be used to deny the public the opportunity to know how members voted on controversial legislation, like pay raise bills.

The Mansfield motion, noted earlier, required a recorded vote (yeas and nays). Article I, §5 of the Constitution requires such a vote on any question, in either house of Congress, whenever demanded by one-fifth of the members present. In the Senate, after a member requests a recorded vote, the presiding officer asks the body whether such a vote is "the desire of one-fifth of those present," and those in support raise their hands. Although the Constitution only requires one-fifth of those present, under Senate practice this has been interpreted to mean at least 11 members — one-fifth of a quorum (51 members). If more than a quorum is present, then more than 11 members are necessary to "second" a call for a roll call vote. In the House, a recorded vote can be obtained in one of two ways: through the constitutionally mandated desire of one-fifth of those present (not necessarily a quorum), and through Rule I, §5(a) which compels a roll call when desired by one-fifth (44 members) of a quorum (218 members).

In the Senate, a recorded vote is accomplished by each member answering the clerk's call of his or her name. In the House, for the most part, recorded votes are taken by use of electronic voting machines into which each member inserts a personal voting card.

In a roll call vote, members of the Congress who are not in attendance can have their view on a particular bill expressed through pairing with members holding opposite views, either present in the chamber (live pair) or absent (dead pair). As can be seen from the roll call on the Mansfield motion to instruct the Judiciary Committee, pairs are not recorded as votes. If a live pair is made, the present legislator cannot cast his or her vote (as Senator Mansfield indicates above: "If I were at liberty to vote, I would vote 'yes'.") In the Senate, absent members can also have their view of a bill expressed by a present member, while in the House, nonpaired (absent) members can only be listed without reference to their preference on a bill.

4.   Reporting a Bill from Committee

Pursuant to the Mansfield motion referring S. 1564 to the Senate Judiciary Committee with instructions, the committee reported the voting rights bill on April 9, 1965, with amendments.

REPORTS OF COMMITTEES

The following reports of committees were submitted:

By Mr. EASTLAND, from the Committee on the Judiciary, with amendments, without recommendation:

S. 1564. A bill to enforce the 15th amendment to the Constitution of the United States (Rept. No. 162).

Usually a committee will make a recommendation to its legislative body with respect to a bill as amended. In this case, the committee made no recommendation. A consensus could not be reached on a number of issues, and the committee was

required to report a bill by April 9. Recall, also, that Senator
Eastland, chair of the committee, was opposed to *every* line of
the legislation. Note also the form in which the bill is reported.
The original bill is reported with amendments. This means that
both the bill and the amendments will be before the parent
chamber. The committee could have reported a "clean" bill,
one with a new number, in which all adopted amendments
had been incorporated. There is no rule that determines which
method a committee will follow on this point. But the form
chosen, as you will see, can make a difference in the way a bill
may be considered, particularly for purposes of subsequent
amendment.

The Congressional Record does not record much about
committee proceedings, only a notice that a committee has reported a bill and the committee's recommendation, if any. To
find out what happened at the committee, including the votes
of its members, one must turn to the committee report, in this
case S. Rep. No. 162 (of the Judiciary Committee), or other
committee records, such as transcripts of committee meetings
(if made) or voting sheets. Committee reports are printed by
the United States Government Printing Office and can be
found, at least in part, in the United States Code Congressional
and Administrative News.

On April 13, 1965, Senator Mansfield moved that the Senate consider the bill, which motion was agreed to by voice
vote.

VOTING RIGHTS ACT OF 1965

Mr. MANSFIELD.   Mr. President, I move that the Senate proceed to the consideration of Calendar No. 149, Senate bill 1564.

The ACTING PRESIDENT pro tempore.   The bill will be stated
by title.

The LEGISLATIVE CLERK.   A bill (S. 1564) to enforce the 15th
amendment of the Constitution of the United States.

The ACTING PRESIDENT pro tempore.   The question is on
agreeing to the motion of the Senator from Montana.

Mr. ELLENDER.   Mr. President, before the question is put, I
should like to ask what the intention of the leadership is.

Mr. MANSFIELD.   The intention is not to debate the bill until
the Senate convenes on April 21.

Mr. ELLENDER.   At 12 o'clock noon on that day.

Mr. MANSFIELD.   At 12 o'clock noon.

Mr. ELLENDER.   No action will be taken in respect to the bill in the mean-time.

Mr. MANSFIELD.   Nothing before that time. There will be a morning hour when we return. Then we shall lay down the bill and again make it the pending business.

The ACTING PRESIDENT pro tempore.   The question is on agreeing to the motion of the Senator from Montana.

The motion was agreed to, and the Senate proceeded to consider the bill, which had been reported from the Committee on the Judiciary with an amendment, to strike out all after the enacting clause and insert: . . .

This motion did not require any immediate action on the bill but only signaled the commencement of its consideration. In fact, later that day, consideration of the bill was resumed and Senator Williams offered an amendment to add certain prohibitions to the bill.

VOTING RIGHTS ACT OF 1965

The Senate resumed the consideration of the bill (S. 1564) to enforce the 15th amendment of the Constitution of the United States.

Mr. WILLIAMS of Delaware.   Mr. President, I understand from the able majority leader that no action will be taken on the pending measure until April 21. However, on behalf of the Senator from Iowa [Mr. Miller] and myself, I send to the desk an amendment and ask that it be stated. I shall discuss the amendment when the Senate reconvenes and I ask that the amendment be made the pending business.

The PRESIDING OFFICER (Mr. Kennedy of New York in the chair).   The amendment will be stated.

The legislative clerk read as follows:

On page 29, line 20, strike all down to and including line 4 on page 30 and insert in lieu the following:

"Whoever knowingly or willfully gives false information as to his name, address, or period of residence in the voting district for the purpose of establishing his eligibility to register or vote, or conspires with another individual for the purpose of encouraging his false registration or illegal voting, or pays or offers to pay or accepts payment either for registration or for voting shall be fined not more than $10,000 or imprisoned not more than five years, or both."

Mr. WILLIAMS of Delaware.   Mr. President, I ask that the amendment just read be made the pending business. I shall discuss it next week.

5. *Floor Amendments*

As noted above, the Judiciary Committee reported S. 1564
to the floor with amendments. In addition to committee
amendments, in Congress, floor amendments are a very important part of the process and are often adopted. This is also
the practice in many states. In some states, floor amendments,
although frequently offered, are almost never adopted due to
strict party discipline. New York is an example of one such
state.

In the Senate, a decision to consider a bill opens the floor
amendment process. In the House, where size requires floor
actions to be far more controlled, the amendatory process is
circumscribed by "rules" from the Rules Committee, which
must be adopted by the House. In either case, the offering of a
floor amendment requires a response from a bill's sponsor or
manager, who, in working to obtain passage of a bill, must decide whether the amendment would kill or substantially reshape the bill or would move the bill toward passage in an
acceptable shape.

Amendments are frequently characterized as either
"friendly" or "hostile" amendments. A friendly amendment,
such as the Williams amendment, is one that is acceptable to a
bill's sponsor, either because it resolves a substantive problem
or furthers its chances for passage. A hostile amendment is one
that is intended to make it impossible to achieve the goals of
the bill's sponsor.

Under the rules of the Senate, an amendment can be offered at any time on any subject, without regard to the germaneness of the amendment to the bill. This procedure creates
opportunities for confusing or obstructing the process. It also
creates opportunities for forcing unpopular votes on senators.
For example, in 1993, members of the Senate, who were opposed to President Clinton's decision to permit gays in the
military, offered an amendment prohibiting such action to the
Home Leave Act of 1992 to create a possible election issue
against those who voted against the amendment. This procedure would have been considered out of order in the House of
Representatives.

To amend a bill in the House the "rule" that governs floor
consideration will set forth the conditions, if any, for amend-

ment. In addition, the House has a standing rule prohibiting nongermane amendments that is in effect unless there is a contrary rule. Whether a particular amendment is germane, of course, is another question that is sometimes quite difficult to resolve.

By introducing his amendment well before commencement of the bill's consideration, Senator Williams chose a tactical path that maximized notice of his intention and his opportunities to garner support for his view. Contrast this tactic with a surprise amendment—one called up for debate on the same day it is introduced—which is frequently intended to slow consideration of a bill or embarrass a member by forcing a vote on a particular issue. The debate on the proposed amendment of Senator Williams started on April 22, 1965.

On April 30, the day after the Williams proposal passed on a roll call vote, the majority and minority leaders, Senators Mansfield and Dirksen, offered an amendment in the form of a substitute for the voting rights legislation.

VOTING RIGHTS ACT OF 1965

The Senate resumed the consideration of the bill (S. 1564) to enforce the 15th amendment of the Constitution of the United States.

Amendment No. 124

Mr. MANSFIELD. Mr. President, on behalf of the distinguished minority leader and myself, I send to the desk a substitute for the voting rights bill which was reported by the Judiciary Committee about 2 weeks ago. The substitute does not differ greatly from the committee bill. On the contrary it recognizes and adopts most of the legal contributions which were made by the distinguished lawyers of the Judiciary Committee. The brilliant work in committee of the able Senator from Michigan [Mr. Hart], the Senator from Missouri [Mr. Long], the Senator from Massachusetts [Mr. Kennedy], the Senator from Indiana [Mr. Bayh], the Senator from North Dakota [Mr. Burdick], the Senator from Maryland [Mr. Tydings], the Senator from Nebraska [Mr. Hruska], the Senator from Hawaii [Mr. Fong], the Senator from Pennsylvania [Mr. Scott], the Senator from New York [Mr. Javits], as well, of course, as that of the distinguished minority leader [Mr. Dirksen]—the great contributions of these Senators to more effective insurance of the right to vote for all, have been, for the most part, retained in the substitute.

The actual changes from the committee version of the bill originally introduced by the joint leadership are not great. I now list them
in summary form.

The first appears in the so-called cleansing portion of the bill,
section 4(a). Our amendment strikes the escape clauses of the present
bill, including the controversial 60 percent escape hatch. In brief, it
provides that a State or subdivision may get out from under the act
only when the effects of the denial and abridgement of the right to
vote have been effectively corrected and there is no reasonable cause
to believe that a test or device will be used for the purpose or will
have the effect of discrimination in voting. As in the present bill, the
court maintains jurisdiction of the matter for 5 years to insure
against backsliding.

In section 7 the substitute simplifies the procedure for listing
voters by Federal examiners. An applicant to an examiner need only
allege that he is not registered and that he has been denied the
opportunity to do so. The Attorney General may waive the latter
requirement.

The amended bill contains a new poll tax provision — section 9
— which is clearly constitutional, which places the Congress clearly
on record against discriminatory poll taxes, and which assures a
speedy determination on the matter by the Supreme Court. It is true
that this provision does not automatically abolish all poll taxes as
some would have the Congress attempt by legislation. But we are
convinced, largely by the arguments of the Attorney General, that
there would be a significant constitutional question involved in such
an attempt. Indeed, it might, in the end, result in no action at all
being taken on poll taxes. We are persuaded, too, that the language
of the substitute not only insures against the use of poll taxes where
there is even the slightest suggestion of discriminatory purpose or
use but also provides for the most rapid and direct court test of the
constitutionality of this question.

Finally, a new section 10 assures that persons listed by Federal
examiners will actually have the ballot placed in their hands.

The amendment proposed by the senior Senator from Delaware
[Mr. Williams], as modified by the senior Senator from North Carolina [Mr. Ervin] and adopted by the Senate yesterday, is included.

The distinguished minority leader and I are in agreement in our
belief that these changes will strengthen the effectiveness of the legislation. We believe they will be helpful in bringing about at the
earliest possible moment the equal treatment of all citizens in their
right to vote in all elections — Federal, State, and local.

I realize that other Members may not feel the same way. Each
lawyer in the Senate as well as all those outside has his own ideas
about how to achieve the same legal purpose. There are many roads

which lead to the same end and they are followed by Senators who are at least as able as the lawyers who worked with us to perfect this substitute. But, in the end, Senators who are generally trying to go in the same direction must also try to get together on the same road, if there is to be any legislation in the Senate at all.

The joint leadership is hopeful that this substitute provides such a road. We are hopeful that, with the key questions now placed in focus, the Senate will proceed steadily until the matter is resolved. For the information of the Senate, it is our intention to consider the substitute at the earliest possible moment consistent with respect for the rights of all other Members. Once it is before the Senate we will stay with it until a decision is made one way or the other. In view of the amount of time already spent on the voting rights legislation, moreover, the Senate is on notice that beginning Monday, sessions will be lengthened. The intention is to come in at noon as heretofore in order to permit committees to meet, on other essential business. But Members should anticipate that the Senate will be in session until about 7 p.m. or later every day. Beginning on Monday the possibility of quorums and votes at any time will exist. Senators should make their plans accordingly.

The PRESIDING OFFICER.   The amendment will be stated.

Note that this amendment was offered by the leadership of both parties of the legislative body. This meant that the bipartisan leadership of the Senate had been spending time negotiating differences with senators to build a majority around compromises reflected in this legislation. This is evident in the comments on the amendment by one of its sponsors, Senator Dirksen.

Mr. DIRKSEN.   I believe the distinguished majority leader has very clearly stated the case. Insofar as possible, we have sought to preserve the text in all sections of the bill that was first offered as it came to the Senate from the committee before the deadline on April 9. We were careful to preserve that language so that it could not be said that we were coming here with an entirely new bill.

However, there were provisions concerning which deep conviction reposed on both sides of the aisle. I come within that orbit of conviction. That concern related, first, to the poll tax; second, with respect to making clear the real objective of the bill; third, with respect to the cleansing provision. Those are the major items as to which modifications have been made. As the majority leader has indicated, we hope that the subject of the poll tax, without actually being resolved in the Senate, and leaving it in the status which it presently enjoys, will finally go to the Supreme Court with as much dispatch as possible for the purpose of obtaining a declaratory judgment.

Then we shall know, notwithstanding the recent decision — in fact, this week — in the Virginia case, and notwithstanding the dicta in that case, where we stand on the subject of the poll tax. I was afraid an impression might go abroad that there was something punitive about the bill and that we were missing the objective of trying to secure the voting rights of people. That was the reason for section 10, verifying and simplifying it, and going to the heart of the subject. Finally, there was the so called cleansing provision in section 4.

Those items constitute the real improvements in the bill. I earnestly hope that when we resume explanation and discussion, not merely today, but in the next week, we can move apace and finally get the bill out of the Senate and on the way to the House of Representatives.

6.   A Legislative Quorum

The debate on the Williams amendment (which occurred before the Mansfield, Dirksen amendment was offered) was interrupted for a quorum call.

Mr. ELLENDER.   Mr. President, I suggest the absence of a quorum.

The PRESIDING OFFICER.   The clerk will call the roll.

The legislative clerk called the roll, and the following Senators answered to their names:

[No. 59 Leg.]

Aiken	Hart	Miller
Bennett	Holland	Mondale
Boggs	Inouye	Monroney
Brewster	Jackson	Mundt
Clark	Javits	Murphy
Cooper	Jordon, ID	Nelson
Cotton	Kuchel	Pastore
Dirksen	Long, MO	Pell
Ellender	Long, LA	Sparkman
Fannin	Mansfield	Tydings
Gruening	McCarthy	Williams, DE
Harris	McNamara	Young, OH

Mr. LONG of Louisiana.   I announce that the Senator from New Mexico [Mr. Anderson], the Senator from Alaska [Mr. Bartlett], the Senator from Tennessee [Mr. Bass], the Senator from Nevada [Mr. Bible], the Senator from Virginia [Mr. Byrd], the Senator from Nevada [Mr. Cannon], the Senator from Connecticut [Mr. Dodd], the Senator from Arkansas [Mr. Fulbright], the Senator from Massachusetts [Mr. Kennedy], the Senator from Washington [Mr. Magnuson], the Senator from Wyoming [Mr. McGee], the Senator from Oregon [Mr. Morse], the Senator from Utah [Mr. Moss], the Senator from Oregon [Mrs. Neuberger], the Senator from Mississippi [Mr. Stennis], the Senator from Texas [Mr. Yarborough] and the Senator from Tennessee [Mr. Gore] are absent on official business. I also announce that the Senator from North Dakota [Mr. Burdick], the Senator from West Virginia [Mr. Byrd], the Senator from Illinois [Mr. Douglas], the Senator from North Carolina [Mr. Jordan], the Senator from Ohio [Mr. Lausche], the Senator from South Dakota [Mr. McGovern], the Senator from New Hampshire [Mr. McIntyre], the Senator from Montana [Mr. Metcalf], the Senator from Maine [Mr. Muskie], the Senator from West Virginia [Mr. Randolph], the Senator from Connecticut [Mr. Ribicoff], the Senator from Georgia [Mr. Russell], the Senator from Florida [Mr. Smathers], the Senator from Missouri [Mr. Symington], and the Senator from Georgia [Mr. Talmadge] are necessarily absent.

Mr. KUCHEL.   I announce that the Senator from Colorado [Mr. Allott], the Senator from Vermont [Mr. Prouty] and the Senator from Massachusetts [Mr. Saltonstall] are necessarily absent.

The Senator from Hawaii [Mr. Fong], the Senator from Iowa [Mr. Hickenlooper], the Senator from Pennsylvania [Mr. Scott] and the Senator from Wyoming [Mr. Simpson] are absent on official business. The Senator from Kansas [Mr. Carlson], the Senator from New Jersey [Mr. Case], the Senator from Nebraska [Mr. Curtis], the Senator from Texas [Mr. Tower], and the Senator from North Dakota [Mr. Young] are detained on official business.

The PRESIDING OFFICER.   A quorum is not present.

Mr. HART.   Mr. President, I move that the Sergeant at Arms be directed to request the attendance of absent Senators.

The PRESIDING OFFICER (Mr. Mondale in the chair).   The question is on agreeing to the motion of the Senator from Michigan.

The motion was agreed to.

The PRESIDING OFFICER.   The Sergeant at Arms will execute the order of the Senate.

After a little delay, Mr. Bayh, Mr. Church, Mr. Dominick, Mr. Eastland, Mr. Ervin, Mr. Hartke, Mr. Hayden, Mr. Hruska, Mr. Kennedy of New York, Mr. McClellan, Mr. Montoya, Mr. Morton, Mr. Proxmire, Mr. Robertson, Mrs. Smith, Mr. Thurmond, and Mr. Williams of New Jersey entered the Chamber and answered to their names.

The PRESIDING OFFICER.   A quorum is present. The Senator from Michigan is recognized.

A quorum is the number of members of a legislative body necessary to be present for the conduct of legislative business. The U.S. Constitution (art. I, §5) requires a quorum of a majority of members to be present to conduct business in either house of Congress. Both houses of Congress operate under the presumption of a quorum's presence, which means that the absence of a quorum must be suggested, through a point of order, by a member. Generally, a member must be recognized to make this point. The consequence of denying such recognition, at least on more than the most infrequent occasions, would almost certainly be chaos. Calling for a quorum has a variety of purposes. First, for purposes of a recorded vote, a quorum call can serve to maximize the number of members whose vote is recorded. Second, all quorum calls take time. Such time can be used to temporarily delay proceedings to negotiate a procedural point or to convince a member to support the legislation. Third, a quorum call can be used to tarnish the attendance record of a member who is not present in the capitol. On occasion, the request for a quorum can result in an adjournment if an insufficient number are available to answer the call. In this case, a quorum was not present, and the Sergeant-at-Arms was instructed to find the absent members.

7.   *Unanimous Consent Agreements*

On May 4, after debates on numerous amendments, Senate Majority Leader Mansfield offered a "unanimous consent agreement" for the purpose of regulating the continuing debate. A request for unanimous consent generally is a request to amend the normal legislative rules for a particular purpose. In the Senate, unanimous consent requests are frequently requests for agreements on the management of the debate on a particular piece of legislation. In this sense they are, if adopted, agreements to limit debate and the freedom of amendment. In the House, this function is served by "rules" from the Committee on Rules (see section C9 of this chapter) and the germaneness rule. In most state legislatures, the function is served by legislative rules limiting debate and requiring germaneness.

In this case the proposed agreement was objected to by Senator Ellender and thus was defeated.

PROPOSED UNANIMOUS-CONSENT AGREEMENT

Mr. MANSFIELD. Mr. President, I send to the desk a proposed unanimous-consent agreement and ask that it be read by the clerk.

The PRESIDING OFFICER.   The clerk will read the proposal.

The legislative clerk read as follows:

Ordered, that at the conclusion of routine morning business on Thursday, May 6, 1965, during the further consideration of S. 1564, debate on the amendment of the senior Senator from North Carolina [Mr. Ervin] shall be limited to 4 hours, to be equally divided and controlled by Senator Ervin and the junior Senator from Michigan [Mr. Hart]: that debate on the amendment to be offered by the junior Senator from Massachusetts [Mr. Kennedy] and others dealing with the poll tax shall be limited to 4 hours, to be equally divided and controlled by the mover of said amendment and the majority leader, and that debate on any other amendment, motion, or appeal, except a motion to lay on the table, shall be limited to 2 hours, to be equally divided and controlled by the mover of any such amendment or motion and the junior Senator from Michigan [Mr. Hart]:

Provided, That in the event the junior Senator from Michigan [Mr. Hart] is in favor of any such amendment or motion, the time in opposition thereto shall be controlled by the majority leader or some Senator designated by him: *Ordered further,* that on the question of the final passage of the said bill, debate shall be limited to 6 hours, to be equally divided and controlled, respectively, by the junior Senator from Michigan [Mr. Hart] and the senior Senator from Louisiana [Mr. Ellender]: *Provided,* That the said leaders, or either of them, may, from the time under their control, on the passage of the said bill, allot additional time to any Senator during the consideration of any amendment, motion, or appeal.

The PRESIDING OFFICER.   Is there objection?

Mr. ELLENDER.   I object.

In response to the objection to the proposed unanimous consent agreement, the majority leader warned the members that the leadership was considering filing a motion for cloture.

VOTING RIGHTS ACT OF 1965

The Senate resumed the consideration of the bill (S. 1564) to enforce the 15th amendment of the Constitution of the United States.

Notice of Possibility of Cloture Motion

Mr. MANSFIELD.   Mr. President, in view of the fact that it seems impossible to arrive at a unanimous consent agreement on the amendments and the bill, I think it is only fair that the leadership should announce at this time, so that all Senators may be informed, that because of the objection raised, we shall have to give very serious consideration to filing a motion for cloture at an appropriate time.

8.   *Filibuster and Cloture*

A filibuster is a delay tactic that takes advantage of the Senate's unlimited debate rule. Cloture is the process for ending a filibuster in the Senate. Under Senate Rule XXII, §2, a motion for cloture requires the signature of 16 senators to be introduced and must be approved by three-fifths of the membership. The need for 60 votes to close debate creates extraordinary power for a large minority of senators to oppose a particular bill through a filibuster and makes particularly powerful a minority party that has greater than 40 members in the Senate. In 1965, at the time of the debate on the Voting Rights Act, the cloture rule required two-thirds of the members or 66 votes of the 100.

After some additional weeks of debate on the bill and various other amendments, on May 21 Senator Hart filed a motion to bring debate on S. 1564 to a close.

VOTING RIGHTS ACT OF 1965

Mr. HART.   Mr. President, I ask unanimous consent that the Chair lay before the Senate the unfinished business.

The ACTING PRESIDENT pro tempore.   The bill will be stated by title.

The LEGISLATIVE CLERK.   A bill (S. 1564) to enforce the 15th amendment to the Constitution of the United States.

The ACTING PRESIDENT pro tempore.   Is there objection?

There being no objection, the Senate resumed the consideration of the bill (S. 1564) to enforce the 15th amendment to the Constitution of the United States.

Cloture Motion

Mr. HART.   Mr. President, I send to the desk a cloture motion filed under rule XXII and ask that it be read.

The ACTING PRESIDENT pro tempore.   The cloture motion will be stated.

The legislative clerk read the motion, as follows:

Cloture Motion

We, the undersigned Senators, in accordance with the provisions of rule XXII of the Standing Rules of the Senate, hereby move to bring to a close the debate upon the bill (S. 1564) to enforce the 15th amendment to the Constitution of the United States.

(1) MIKE MANSFIELD; (2) EVERETT M. DIRKSEN; (3) PHILIP A. HART; (4) THOMAS H. KUCHEL; (5) LEVERETT SALTONSTALL; (6) PAT McNAMARA; (7) JOHN O. PASTORE; (8) FRANK E. MOSS; (9) JACOB K. JAVITS; (10) HUGH SCOTT; (11) HIRAM L. FONG; (12) CLAIBORNE PELL; (13) EDMUND S. MUSKIE; (14) WAYNE MORSE; (15) JOHN SHERMAN COOPER; (16) STEPHEN M. YOUNG; (17) CLIFFORD P. CASE; (18) EUGENE J. McCARTHY; (19) WALTER F. MONDALE; (20) DANIEL BREWSTER; (21) FRED R. HARRIS; (22) DANIEL K. INOUYE; (23) PAUL H. DOUGLAS; (24) JOSEPH S. CLARK; (25) GAYLORD NELSON; (26) JENNINGS RANDOLPH; (27) ABRAHAM RIBICOFF; (28) FRANK J. LAUSCHE; (29) THOMAS J. DODD; (30) VANCE HARTKE; (31) JOSEPH D. TYDINGS; (32) EDWARD V. LONG; (33) BIRCH BAYH; (34) EDWARD KENNEDY; (35) LEE METCALF; (36) GORDON ALLOTT; (37) HARRISON WILLIAMS; (38) QUENTIN BURDICK.

Mr. HART subsequently said: Mr. President, on behalf of the junior Senator from New Jersey [Mr. Williams] and the junior Senator from North Dakota [Mr. Burdick], I ask unanimous consent that their signatures may be permitted to be added to the cloture motion filed today under rule XXII with respect to the voting rights bill.

The ACTING PRESIDENT pro tempore.   Without objection, it is so ordered.

Mr. ALLOTT subsequently said: Mr. President, I ask unanimous consent that my signature may be added to the cloture motion notwithstanding the fact that it has already been filed.

The ACTING PRESIDENT pro tempore.   Without objection, it is so ordered.

This motion was adopted on May 25. It was only the second time, after a long history of defeating civil rights legislation through filibustering, that debate had been forcibly closed. On May 26, 1965, the Senate adopted by roll call vote the Mansfield-Dirksen substitute, as amended, for the committee substitute for the bill; it then adopted by voice vote the committee amendment in the nature of a substitute as amended by the Mansfield-Dirksen substitute; finally, it adopted by roll call vote S. 1564 as so amended.

9.   *Governing the House Debate: Rules Committee and Its Rules*

Floor action on the voting rights issue resumed in the House of Representatives on June 1, 1965, when H.R. 6400, as amended and having passed the Committee on the Judiciary, was referred to the Committee of the Whole House of the State of the Union (Committee of the Whole) under a "rule" from the House Committee on Rules. This Committee of the Whole is the subject of the next section of this chapter. The scheduling of legislation for the Committee of the Whole (and usually in the House itself) is up to the House Rules Committee, which is responsible for scheduling consideration of legislation and for the terms for such consideration. There is a rules committee in the Senate and almost all houses of state legislatures, but, for the most part, they serve other functions that need not be addressed here.

The committee's instrument for communicating its determination is a *rule*. Such a rule is distinct from the standing rules of the House and functions as the procedural guide under which a particular piece of legislation will be considered. The authority to control scheduling and procedure makes this committee extremely powerful.

The sponsor of the bill or the chair of the substantive committee that reported the bill (in this case, the Committee on the Judiciary) begins the process by requesting a rule from the Rules Committee chair. If the Rules Committee, mostly through its chairperson, agrees to proceed with this request, hearings generally are held. If it does not, the bill most frequently is killed.

Hearings before the Rules Committee usually include discussion of the substance of the bill as well as discussion of the terms of debate. The Rules Committee cannot amend a bill, but it can express its view of the bill by the rule it fashions, including authorizing the consideration of particular amendments, by not granting a rule, or by recommending that the bill be recommitted to the substantive committee. The committee can also trade a rule for changes in the bill.

A rule from the Rules Committee, in the form of a House Resolution (H.R. Res.) must be approved by the House prior to the commencement of the consideration of the bill that the rule addresses. In effect, it is treated as a separate piece of legislation.

VOTING RIGHTS ACT OF 1965

Mr. BOLLING.   Mr. Speaker, by direction of the Committee on Rules, I call up a resolution (H. Res. 440) and ask for its immediate consideration.

The Clerk reads as follows:

H. Res. 440

Resolved, That upon the adoption of this resolution it shall be in order to move that the House resolve itself into the Committee of the Whole House on the State of the Union for the consideration of the bill (H.R. 6400) to enforce the fifteenth amendment to the Constitution of the United States. After general debate, which shall be confined to the bill and shall continue not to exceed ten hours, to be equally divided and controlled by the chairman and ranking minority member of the Committee on the Judiciary, the bill shall be read for amendment under the five-minute rule. It shall be in order to consider the amendment in the nature of a substitute recommended by the Committee on the Judiciary now in the bill and such amendment shall be considered under the five-minute rule as an original bill for the purpose of amendment. It shall also be in order to consider the text of the bill H.R. 7896 as a substitute for the committee amendment in the nature of a substitute printed in the bill. At the conclusion of such consideration the Committee shall rise and report the bill to the House with such amendments as may have been adopted, and any Member may demand a separate vote in the House on any of the amendments adopted in the Committee of the Whole to the bill or the committee amendment in the nature of a substitute. The previous question shall be considered as ordered on the bill and amendments thereto to final passage without intervening motion except one motion to recommit with or without instructions. After the passage of the bill H.R. 6400, it shall be in order in the House to take from the Speaker's table the bill S. 1564 and to move to strike out all after the enacting clause of said Senate bill and to insert in lieu thereof the provisions contained in H.R. 6400 as passed by the House.

There are basically three types of rules: open, closed, and modified closed. All of the rules fix the time for general debate on the bill. Under an open rule, the most typical and the type granted for H.R. 6400, any germane amendment, simple or complex, may be offered after the general debate has occurred. Under H.R. Res. 440, such amendments in the Committee of the Whole cannot be discussed for longer than the five-minute rule. A member may speak in favor of his or her amendment for five minutes, and an opponent has five minutes to reply. In practice, debate over an amendment can last significantly longer by a successful request for unanimous consent to continue or by a motion to "strike out the last word" of the amendment under debate. This latter motion is a ploy that permits continued debate on the same amendment (minus its last word). Closed rules prohibit floor amendments. They are controversial because they contradict the democratic values of the House. They are used in certain cases to force a yes or no vote, only on a particular bill. Modified closed rules are a cross between open and closed rules, with some parts of the bill open to amendment and other parts closed.

Within these broad contours, the Rules Committee can be quite creative in fashioning particular rules to effect various goals. In addition to authorizing an open amendment period, H.R. Res. 440 contained additional instructions, relating to the treatment of certain proposed amendments. As noted earlier, the Judiciary Committee had proposed an amendment in the nature of a substitute. H.R. Res. 440 allowed the committee substitute to be treated as the original bill, which meant that it, and not the original bill, was the bill that would be the subject of debate and proposed amendments. Two Republicans were also specially authorized to offer H.R. 7896 as a substitute amendment to the committee's bill. This effectively meant that the amendment could be considered outside the five-minute

rule. Most likely this special treatment was part of an agreement with supporters in the minority party (Republicans) that
gave them an opportunity to present a somewhat different bill
for consideration in return for support of the committee substitute, if their amendment did not pass. (As noted later, this
amendment failed, and both of its sponsors supported the
committee substitute).

   H.R. Res. 440 was approved by the House on July 6, 1965,
by a voice vote. While the adoption of a rule by the House,
particularly an open rule, is usually perfunctory, sometimes
the consideration of a rule precipitates a major fight, either on
the terms of the rule or on the substance of the legislation to
which the rule is addressed. If the motion to cut off such debate is defeated, sponsors of the underlying legislation frequently will withdraw the bill for further coalition-building.
An example of major fight over a rule was the battle that sur-
rounded the 1994 federal crime bill. The rule was defeated and
the bill replaced by one much more palatable to its opponents.
For an in-depth study of the Rules Committee, its processes,
and its products, see Walter Oleszek, Congressional Procedures and the Policy Process (1989); S. Bach and S. S. Smith,
Managing Uncertainty in the House of Representatives (1988);
Charles Tiefer, Congressional Practice and Procedure (1989).

10.   The Committee of the Whole House on the State of the Union

   All bills that involve a tax, an appropriation, or the authorization of an appropriation (almost all bills) are by House
rules referred to the Committee of the Whole House on the
State of the Union (the Committee of the Whole). The Committee of the Whole is, in effect, the House of Representatives
operating under some different procedures designed, in part,
to make the consideration of bills more efficient. All representatives are members, but a quorum consists of only 100
members instead of the 218 required for the House. A recorded
vote needs 25 members. The Committee of the Whole is where
the House debate occurs and where amendments are offered.

   When the House constitutes itself as the Committee of the
Whole, the Speaker steps down as presiding officer and is re-

placed by the chair of the Committee of the Whole, a member so designated by the Speaker. This action is accompanied by the removal of the Speaker's mace (a traditional symbol of the Speaker's authority consisting of a bundle of 13 ebony rods bound in silver, topped with a silver globe and a silver eagle). Both of these acts are rooted in the historically close relationship between the English kings and parliamentary speakers and the determination of the House of Commons during the rule of King John to create a forum in which debate could occur outside of the King's "ears."

Pursuant to the rule, general debate commenced in the Committee of the Whole on July 6, 1965.

Mr. CELLER. Mr. Speaker, I move that the House resolve itself into the Committee of the Whole House on the State of the Union for the consideration of the bill (H.R. 6400) to enforce the 15th amendment to the Constitution of the United States.

The SPEAKER. The question is on the motion offered by the gentleman from New York.

The motion was agreed to.

IN THE COMMITTEE OF THE WHOLE

Accordingly, the House resolved itself into the Committee of the Whole House on the State of the Union for the consideration of the bill H.R. 6400, with Mr. Bolling in the chair.

The Clerk read the title of the bill.

By unanimous consent, the first reading of the bill was dispensed with.

The CHAIRMAN. Under the rule, the gentleman from New York [Mr. Celler], will be recognized for 5 hours, and the gentleman from Ohio [Mr. McCulloch], will be recognized for 5 hours. The Chair recognizes the gentleman from New York.

Mr. CELLER. Mr. Chairman, I yield myself such time as I may consume.

Debate in legislative bodies serves various purposes, only one of which is occasionally affecting the vote of members who remain undecided at that time. Professor Oleszek sums it up nicely.

General debate is both symbolic and practical. It assures both legislators and the public that the House makes its decision in a democratic fashion, with due respect for majority and minority opinions. "Debate appropriately tests the conclusions of the majority." General debate forces members to come to grips with the issues at hand; difficult and controversial sections of the bill are explained; constituents and interest groups are alerted to a measure's purpose through press coverage of the debate; member sentiment can be assessed by the floor leaders; a public record, or legislative history, for administrative agencies and the courts is built, revealing the intentions of the proponents and opponents alike; legislators may take positions for reelection purposes; and, occasionally, fence-sitters may be influenced.

Not all legislators agree on the last point. Some doubt that debate can really change views or affect the outcome of a vote. But debate, especially by party leaders just before a key vote, can change opinion. . . .

In sum, reasoned deliberation is important in decision making. Lawmaking consists of more than log rolling, compromises, or power plays. General debate enables members to gain a better understanding of complex issues, and it may influence the collective decision of the House.

Walter Oleszek, Congressional Procedures and the Policy Process 149 (1989).

The ten-hour debate on H.R. 6400 was held over a three-day period. On July 8, after general debate had ended, the amendment process began. In the House, this is normally done on a section by section basis starting with the enactment clause. In this manner, amendments are offered after the section to which they relate has been read. Under the rule, it was in order for the House to consider H.R. 7896 (Ford-McCulloch) as a substitute for the committee amendment in the nature of a substitute. No time for such consideration was explicit in the rule, but two hours were agreed to by unanimous consent of the Committee of the Whole.

The CHAIRMAN.   All time has expired. The Clerk will read. The Clerk read as follows:

Be it enacted by the Senate and House of Representatives of the United States of America in Congress assembled, That this Act shall be known as the "Voting Rights Act of 1965."

AMENDMENT OFFERED BY MR. McCULLOCH

Mr. McCULLOCH.   Mr. Chairman, I offer an amendment.

The Clerk read as follows:

Amendment offered by Mr. McCULLOCH as a substitute for the committee amendment:

Mr. McCULLOCH (interrupting the reading).   Mr. Chairman, I ask unanimous consent that further reading of the amendment be dispensed with, and that the amendment be printed in the RECORD and be open for amendment at any point.

The CHAIRMAN.   Is there objection to the request of the gentleman from Ohio?

There was no objection.

Mr. CELLER.   Mr. Chairman, I ask unanimous consent that all debate on the so-called McCulloch substitute and all amendments thereto be limited to 2 hours, and that such time be equally divided and controlled by myself and the gentleman from Ohio [Mr. McCulloch].

The CHAIRMAN.   Is there objection to the request of the gentleman from New York?

There was no objection.

On July 9, 1965, H.R. 7896, which had been amended, was defeated on a teller vote.

The amendment process continued throughout the day, with some amendments adopted and some rejected. One amendment, offered by Representative Cramer, illustrates the value of different forms of nonrecorded voting, as a ruling of the chair was overturned by a teller vote.

The CHAIRMAN.   The time of the gentleman has expired. All time has expired. The question is on the amendment offered by the gentleman from Florida. The question was taken; and the Chairman announced that the noes appeared to have it.

Mr. CRAMER.   Mr. Chairman, I demand tellers.

Tellers were ordered and the Chairman appointed as tellers Mr. CRAMER and Mr. RODINO. The Committee divided and the tellers reported that there were — ayes 136, noes 132.

The amendment was agreed to.

At 7:20 P.M. on July 9, 1965, with debate concluded in the Committee of the Whole, a voice vote on H.R. 6400 (as amended by the Judiciary Committee and by the Committee of the Whole) was taken, the amended bill was adopted, the Committee of the Whole rose, the Speaker took the rostrum, and the bill was ready for consideration by the House.

The CHAIRMAN.   All debate is concluded even with a preferential motion. The agreement was that all debate would conclude at 7:20 P.M. The hour is now 7:20 P.M. There is no further time.

The question is on the committee amendment, as amended.

The committee amendment, as amended, was agreed to.

Mr. GERALD R. FORD.   Mr. Chairman, a parliamentary inquiry.

The CHAIRMAN.   The gentleman will state his parliamentary inquiry.

Mr. GERALD R. FORD.   At what point in this process will we have an opportunity to ask for separate votes on the Cramer vote-fraud amendment and on the Boggs amendment?

The CHAIRMAN.   In the House, after the previous question has been announced by the Speaker.

Under the rule, the Committee rises.

Accordingly, the Committee rose; and the Speaker having resumed the chair, Mr. BOLLING, Chairman of the Committee of the Whole House on the State of the Union, reported that Committee having had under consideration the bill (H.R. 6400) to enforce the 15th amendment to the Constitution of the United States, pursuant to House Resolution 440, he reported the bill back to the House with an amendment adopted in the Committee of the Whole.

The SPEAKER.   Under the rule, the previous question is ordered.

Is a separate vote demanded on any amendment to the committee amendment?

---

11.   A Bill on the Floor of the House

After the Committee of the Whole has completed its work, including the amendment process, the bill moves to the House for final action. In the House, members must first consider any amendments approved by the Committee of the Whole and then consider the bill in its reported or amended form. New amendments may not be offered nor may amendments defeated in the Committee of the Whole be offered. A motion to recommit the bill with or without instruction on what is to be reconsidered, if the bill is recommitted, is then in order. This recommittal motion gives the opposition one last chance to reshape or to kill the bill. In this instance, the Cramer amendment was adopted, and two remaining ones were rejected. After the amendments adopted by the Committee of the

Whole were disposed of, pursuant to the rule, the House turned to the amendment of the Judiciary Committee that had been considered in the Committee of the Whole along with the original version of H.R. 6400. This amendment was adopted, and the House was ready for action on H.R. 6400 as amended.

The SPEAKER.   The question is on the committee amendment as amended.

The committee amendment as amended was agreed to.

The SPEAKER.   The question is on engrossment and third reading of the bill.

The bill was ordered to be engrossed and read a third time and was read the third time.

MOTION TO RECOMMIT BY MR. COLLIER

Mr. COLLIER.   Mr. Speaker, I offer a motion to recommit.

The SPEAKER.   Is the gentleman opposed to the bill?

Mr. COLLIER.   In its present form I am, Mr. Speaker.

The SPEAKER.   The gentleman qualifies.

The Clerk will report the motion to recommit.

Notice in the Speaker's call of the question the reference to the engrossed bill and third reading. An engrossed bill is the final copy of the bill passed by either house (with all of the adopted amendments) certified by that house's clerk. The engrossed bill and its uses are discussed more fully in Chapter Five, page 176. Each bill in Congress and in state legislatures is supposed to be read three times before passage. This procedure reflects an earlier history when many members of legislatures could not read. In modern practice, bills are not read aloud three times, although in the House, they may be read once in the Committee of the Whole.

After the motion to recommit was defeated on a recorded vote, H.R. 6400 (as amended) was adopted on a recorded vote by the House. Immediately thereafter, in accordance with the terms of the rule, the House amended the Senate bill (S. 1564) by replacing everything following its enacting clause with the text of the House bill.

Mr. CELLER.   Mr. Speaker, pursuant to House Resolution 440, I call up from the Speaker's table for immediate consideration the bill

S. 1564, an act to enforce the 15th amendment to the Constitution of the United States, and for other purposes.

The Clerk read the title of the bill.

AMENDMENT OFFERED BY MR. CELLER

Mr. CELLER.   Mr. Speaker, I offer an amendment.

The Clerk read as follows:

Amendment offered by Mr. CELLER: Strike out all after the enacting clause of S. 1564 and insert in lieu thereof the text of H.R. 6400, as passed.

The amendment was agreed to.

The bill was ordered to be read a third time, was read the third time, and passed.

The title was amended so as to read: "A bill to enforce the 15th amendment to the Constitution of the United States, and for other purposes."

This process of amendment in effect created a single bill, S. 1564, which had been acted upon by both houses, but it did not resolve the substantive disagreements between the version adopted by the Senate and the one adopted by the House; rather it set the stage for the next step in the legislative process. On July 12, 1965, the Senate requested a conference, after it rejected the House-amended version of S. 1564.

ENFORCEMENT OF THE 15TH AMENDMENT TO THE CONSTITUTION

Mr. MANSFIELD.   Mr. President, I ask the Chair to lay before the Senate the amendments of the House of Representatives to the bill (S. 1564).

The PRESIDING OFFICER laid before the Senate the amendments of the House of Representatives to the bill (S. 1564) to enforce the 15th amendment to the Constitution of the United States, and for other purposes, which were, to strike out all after the enacting clause and insert: . . .

Mr. MANSFIELD.   Mr. President, I move that the Senate disagree to the amendments of the House to the bill (S. 1564) and request a conference on the disagreeing votes of the two Houses, and that conferees on the part of the Senate be appointed by the Chair.

The motion was agreed to; and the Presiding Officer appointed Mr. Eastland, Mr. Dodd, Mr. Hart, Mr. Long of Missouri, Mr. Dirksen, and Mr. Hruska conferees on the part of the Senate.

12.   The Conference

The conference is the means by which the two houses of Congress resolve the differences between them on a bill that both houses have considered and adopted. Such agreement is necessary if a bill is to become law because each house must pass an identical version of the same bill. The House Speaker and the presiding officer of the Senate name conferees to the conference committee. Conferees are usually members of the substantive committee that reported the legislation and are recommended by the committee chair and ranking minority member. A conference report must be approved by a majority of the conferees from each house; it does not matter how many members are appointed from each house, although it may change the dynamics of arriving at an intrahouse compromise.

In many instances, although not in this case, conferees are instructed on the position they are to take at a conference committee; these instructions, however, do not strictly bind them. Conferees are not authorized to address provisions of the bill that are not in dispute in the bill. However, during the bargaining process that goes on in the conference, other issues can be put on the table, even if not in dispute in the bill or germane to the bill. An extreme example of using the conference to bring an unrelated issue to the table is recalled by one of the authors, Judge Mikva. In the mid-1970s, each house of Congress had passed a different bill amending the social security law. A conference committee was established, chaired by Representative Al Ullman, chair of the House Ways and Means Committee. A meeting was scheduled during the Christmas vacation because of the urgency of the social security issue. Senator Russell Long, a member of the conference committee and chair of the Senate Finance Committee, opened the conference by informing the members from the House that he was concerned about a piece of legislation, sponsored by a Senate colleague, dealing with tuition tax credits for parochial schools. This bill had been bottled up by Representative

Ullman in the House Ways and Means Committee. Simply stated, Senator Long insisted that the bill be moved as a cost of reaching an agreement on social security. After this request was rejected, the conference was adjourned. A number of days later, as time started to run out, Long agreed to proceed with the conference and drop his intransigence if Ullman could win approval for such action from the Senate colleague whose bill was being held. After such approval was granted, a conference report was negotiated and adopted. Sometime later, it was reported to Representative Mikva, who had been a member of the conference committee, that the object of Long's ploy had not been his colleague's bill but rather another bill, on oil taxes, that he was trying to have moved in the Ways and Means Committee. For a detailed description of the working of conference committees, see L.D. Longley and W.J. Oleszek, Bicameral Politics and the Conference Committees (1989).

When a conference committee reaches an agreement, it issues a conference report that details the agreement. This report then becomes the vehicle for further legislative action. It may contain exact bill language, but it may only contain references to prior legislative action, such as an amendment of one house or the other. The report is then considered by the house that accepted the request for a conference (in this case, the House, which agreed to the conference on July 14). The report is not subject to amendment and, if not adopted by both houses, it must go back to another conference. When both houses agree to a conference report, that report becomes the mandate for the bill's enrollment.

The conference report on S. 1564, as amended, was called up in the House of Representatives on August 3, 1965.

VOTING RIGHTS

Mr. CELLER.   Mr. Speaker, I call up the conference report on the bill (S. 1564) to enforce the 15th amendment to the Constitution of the United States, and for other purposes, and ask unanimous consent that the statement of the managers on the part of the House be read in lieu of the report.

The Clerk read the title of the bill.

The SPEAKER.   Is there objection to the request of the gentlemen from New York?

There was no objection.

The Clerk read the statement.

The conference report and statement are as follows:

Conference Report
(Rept. No. 711)

The committee of conference on the disagreeing votes of the two Houses on the amendment of the House to the bill (S. 1564) to enforce the fifteenth amendment to the Constitution of the United States, and for other purposes, having met, after full and free conference, have agreed to recommend and do recommend to their respective Houses as follows:

That the Senate recede from its disagreement to the amendment of the House to the substantive provisions of the bill and agree to the same with an amendment as follows: In lieu of the matter proposed to be inserted by the House amendment insert the following:

"That this Act shall be known as the 'Voting Rights Act of 1965.' . . ."

The House adopted the Conference Report on August 3, and the Senate followed on August 4. The bill, now passed by both houses, was ready for presidential action. Before a bill can be sent to the president, it has to be enrolled (produced as a final copy), printed on parchment and certified by the clerk of the house of origin (the Senate, in this case), and signed by both the Speaker of the House and the Senate president pro tempore. In the House, the Committee on House Administration is charged with responsibility for verifying the bill, prior to the Speaker signing it. The enrollment process is described more fully in Chapter Five, section A. On August 6, 1965, President Johnson signed the enrolled S. 1564, and the Voting Rights Act of 1965 became law.

13. *Executive Approval or Veto*

The U.S. Constitution and the constitutions of all states (except North Carolina) require bills passed by both house of the legislature to be presented to the executive for approval or veto. The veto power is not absolute; a supermajority of legislators in each legislative chamber may override a veto. The U.S. Constitution's language is typical:

>   Every Bill which shall have passed the House of Represen-
> tatives and the Senate, shall, before it becomes a Law, be pre-
> sented to the President of the United States; If he approve he
> shall sign it, but if not he shall return it, with his Objections to
> that House in which it shall have originated, who shall enter the
> Objections at large on their Journal, and proceed to reconsider
> it. If after such Reconsideration two thirds of that House shall
> agree to pass the Bill, it shall be sent, together with the
> Objections, to the other House, by which it shall likewise be
> reconsidered, and if approved by two thirds of that House, it
> shall become a Law. But in all such Cases the Votes of both
> Houses shall be determined by Yeas and Nays, and the Names
> of the Persons voting for and against the Bill shall be entered on
> the Journal of each House respectively. If any Bill shall not be
> returned by the President within ten Days (Sundays excepted)
> after it shall have been presented to him, the Same shall be a
> Law, in the like Manner as if he had signed it, unless the
> Congress by their Adjournment prevent its Return, in which
> Case it shall not be a Law.

U.S. Const. art. I, §7, cl.2.

The executive veto is the most important external check on legislative activity. "It establishes a salutary check upon the legislative body, calculated to guard the community against the effects of faction, precipitancy, or of any impulse un-friendly to the public good, which may happen to influence a majority of that body." The Federalist No. 73, at 495 (Alex-ander Hamilton) (Jacob E. Cooke ed., 1961). Hamilton thought its use would be infrequent: "It is evident that there would be greater danger of his not using his power when necessary, than of his using it too often, or too much." Id. at 497. Recent presidents, however, have used or threatened to use the power with some frequency.

In modern practice, the exercise of the veto power has not signaled executive displeasure with the legislative process but rather with the legislative product. No executive objects to the "precipitous" passage of legislation he or she favors. In the age of statutes, presidents increasingly have participated vigorous-ly in the legislative process by drafting legislation and lobby-ing for its adoption. The veto power has added special weight to their participation. Through the veto power the president becomes a "third branch of the legislature." Woodrow Wilson, Congressional Government 53 (Johns Hopkins ed. 1981).

Most state constitutions also grant governors the power to exercise vetoes on parts of a bill rather than on the bill as a whole. This is known as the *item veto*. The term is inclusive, intended to cover the power to veto amounts of appropriations (the most typical), the language of appropriations bills, or the language of nonappropriations bills (for example, in the state of Washington). The term also covers what is known as the *amendatory veto*, the power of the governor to condition the approval of bill on the enactment by the legislature of recommended amendments. Each of these powers makes the executive a more significant player in the legislative process than the general veto power does alone. Each of these powers also creates additional opportunities for court involvement in the legislative process.

In 1996, following nearly a century of steadfastly rejecting proposals to constitutionally provide line item veto authority to the president, Congress, as a consequence of an intense political debate surrounding the federal deficit, enacted the Line Item Veto Act (effective January 1, 1997), under which presidents are granted line item veto authority over appropriations, new direct spending, and certain tax benefits. The statute is less than it seems. The authority given the president is statutory not constitutional. This means two things: first that it is subject to constitutional challenge and, second, that it is subject to statutory change. On the former point, a federal district court has declared that the act violates Article I, §1 of the Constitution, which grants "[a]ll legislative powers" to Congress, and Article I, §7 (the Presentment Clause). Byrd v. Raines, 957 F. Supp. 25 (D.D.C. 1997). (The Supreme Court vacated the judgment in this case and ordered the complaint dismissed after holding that petitioners were without standing. Raines v. Byrd, 1997 U.S. LEXIS 4040.) On the latter point, Congress could circumvent the law by simply adding to any bill language declaring that a particular act, title, section, or item shall not be subject to provisions of the Line Item Veto Act.

Once a bill is presented to the executive, copies normally are sent to executive departments interested in the legislation. These departments provide their view of what action the executive should take. Most such executive departments will be quite familiar with the legislation because they may have authored the original bill or lobbied for it in some fashion during the enactment process. Additional lobbying efforts will be made by other interested parties. In the end, the executive weighs all of this argumentation along with his or her own policy and political views and arrives at a decision.

It is important to stress that the Voting Rights Act of 1965 was an executive legislative initiative, and both he and his staff, along with the Justice Department, were deeply involved in the movement of the bill through the legislative process. For a fuller discussion of the veto and line item veto, see Abner J. Mikva and Eric Lane, Legislative Process 649-709 (1995).

CHAPTER FOUR

The Anatomy of a Statute

In Chapter One we address the methods by which courts interpret statutes, and in Chapters Two and Three we outline the processes by which legislatures enact them. In this chapter, the focus is on the anatomy of a statute: its language, form, and elements. By elements we mean the title and enacting clause, found in every statute, and various generic provisions that are common to most statutes. Examples of generic provisions are short titles, findings, definitions, sanctions, severability clauses, and effective dates.

An example of a federal statute follows. It is an excerpted version of a statute that is popularly known as the National Voter Registration Act of 1993. (This statute is informally known as the "Motor Voter" Act.) The excerpt includes the generic statutory provisions, referred to above, and enough of the statute's substance to generally inform of the requirements of the new law. Excluded is much of its detail, although all of its section headings are included. The form of the statute is that found in the collection of federal statutes called Statutes at Large. Basically, this form is an exact copy of the enrolled bill, the bill that actually becomes law. Statutes at Large and enrolled bills are described in Chapter Five. We have added certain descriptive phrases to the statute for identification purposes. They are in bold font and bracketed and are not part of the statute. These bracketed sections, along with other types of statutory provisions, are discussed in section B of this chapter.

A.   AN EXAMPLE OF A STATUTE — NATIONAL VOTER REGISTRATION ACT OF 1993

NATIONAL VOTER REGISTRATION ACT OF 1993

[Designation]

Pub. L. No. 103-31
103d Congress

AN ACT

[Title]

To establish national voter registration procedures for Federal elections, and for other purposes.

[Enactment Clause]

Be it enacted by the Senate and House of Representatives of the United States of America in Congress assembled,

[Short Title]

SECTION 1. SHORT TITLE

This Act may be cited as the "National Voter Registration Act of 1993."

[Legislative Findings and Purposes]

SEC. 2. FINDINGS AND PURPOSES

(a) FINDINGS —. The Congress finds that —
    (1) the right of citizens of the United States to vote is a fundamental right;

(2) it is the duty of the Federal, State, and local governments to promote the exercise of that right; and

(3) discriminatory and unfair registration laws and procedures can have a direct and damaging effect on voter participation in elections for Federal office and disproportionately harm voter participation by various groups, including racial minorities.

(b) PURPOSES. — The purposes of this Act are —

(1) to establish procedures that will increase the number of eligible citizens who register to vote in elections for Federal office;

(2) to make it possible for Federal, State, and local governments to implement this Act in a manner that enhances the participation of eligible citizens as voters in elections for Federal office;

(3) to protect the integrity of the electoral process; and

(4) to ensure that accurate and current voter registration rolls are maintained.

[Definitions]

SEC. 3. DEFINITIONS.

As used in this Act —

(1) the term "election" has the meaning stated in section 301(1) of the Federal Election Campaign Act of 1971 (2 U.S.C. §431(1));

(2) the term "Federal office" has the meaning stated in section 301(3) of the Federal Election Campaign Act of 1971 (2 U.S.C. §431(3));

(3) the term "motor vehicle driver's license" includes any personal identification document issued by a State motor vehicle authority;

(4) the term "State" means a State of the United States and the District of Columbia; and

(5) the term "voter registration agency" means an office designated under section 7(a)(1) to perform voter registration activities.

[Changes in Law]

SEC. 4. NATIONAL PROCEDURES FOR VOTER REGISTRATION FOR ELECTIONS FOR FEDERAL OFFICE

(a) IN GENERAL. — Except as provided in subsection (b), notwithstanding any other Federal or State law, in addition to any other method of voter registration provided for under State law, each State shall establish procedures to register to vote in elections for Federal office —

(1) by application made simultaneously with an application for a motor vehicle driver's license pursuant to section 5;

(2) by mail application pursuant to section 6; and

(3) by application in person —

(A) at the appropriate registration site designated with respect to the residence of the applicant in accordance with State law; and

(B) at a Federal, State, or nongovernmental office designated under section 7.

(b) NONAPPLICABILITY TO CERTAIN STATES. — This Act does not apply to a State described in either or both of the following paragraphs:

(1) A State in which, under law that is in effect continuously on and after March 11, 1993, there is no voter registration requirement for any voter in the State with respect to an election for Federal office.

(2) A State in which under law that is in effect continuously on and after March 11, 1993, or that was enacted on or prior to March 11, 1993, and by its terms is to come into effect upon the enactment of this Act, so long as that law remains in effect, all voters in the State may register to vote at the polling place at the time of voting in a general election for Federal office.

SEC. 5. SIMULTANEOUS APPLICATION FOR VOTER REGISTRATION AND APPLICATION FOR MOTOR VEHICLE DRIVER'S LICENSE

(a) IN GENERAL. — (1) Each State motor vehicle driver's

license application (including any renewal application) submitted to the appropriate State motor vehicle authority under State law shall serve as an application for voter registration with respect to elections for Federal office unless the applicant fails to sign the voter registration application. . . .

SEC. 6. MAIL REGISTRATION

(a) FORM. — (1) Each State shall accept and use the mail voter registration application form prescribed by the Federal Election Commission pursuant to section 9(a)(2) for the registration of voters in elections for Federal office. . . .

SEC. 7. VOTER REGISTRATION AGENCIES

(a) DESIGNATION. — (1) Each State shall designate agencies for the registration of voters in elections for Federal office.

(2) Each State shall designate as voter registration agencies —

(A) all offices in the State that provide public assistance; and

(B) all offices in the State that provide State-funded programs primarily engaged in providing services to persons with disabilities. . . .

SEC. 8. REQUIREMENTS WITH RESPECT TO ADMINISTRATION OF VOTER REGISTRATION . . .

SEC. 9. FEDERAL COORDINATION AND REGULATIONS . . .

SEC. 10. DESIGNATION OF CHIEF STATE ELECTION OFFICIAL

Each State shall designate a State officer or employee as the chief State election official to be responsible for coordination of State responsibilities under this Act.

[Remedies and Sanctions]

SEC. 11. CIVIL ENFORCEMENT AND PRIVATE RIGHT OF ACTION

(a) ATTORNEY GENERAL. — The Attorney General may bring a civil action in an appropriate district court for such declaratory or injunctive relief as is necessary to carry out this Act.

(b) PRIVATE RIGHT OF ACTION. — (1) A person who is aggrieved by a violation of this Act may provide written notice of the violation to the chief election official of the State involved. . . .

(c) ATTORNEY'S FEES. — In a civil action under this section, the court may allow the prevailing party (other than the United States) reasonable attorney fees, including litigation expenses, and costs.

(d) RELATION TO OTHER LAWS. — (1) The rights and remedies established by this section are in addition to all other rights and remedies provided by law, and neither the rights and remedies established by this section nor any other provision of this Act shall supersede, restrict, or limit the application of the Voting Rights Act of 1965 (42 U.S.C. §§1973 et seq.). . . .

SEC. 12. CRIMINAL PENALTIES

A person, including an election official, who in any election for Federal office —

(1) knowingly and willfully intimidates, threatens, or coerces, or attempts to intimidate, threaten, or coerce, any person for —

(A) registering to vote, or voting, or attempting to register or vote;

(B) urging or aiding any person to register to vote, to vote, or to attempt to register or vote; or

(C) exercising any right under this Act; or

(2) knowingly and willfully deprives, defrauds, or attempts to deprive or defraud the residents of a State of a fair and impartially conducted election process, by —

(A) the procurement or submission of voter registration applications that are known by the person to be materially false, fictitious, or fraudulent under the laws of the State in which the election is held; or

    (B) the procurement, casting, or tabulation of ballots that are known by the person to be materially false, fictitious or fraudulent under the laws of the State in which the election is held,

shall be fined in accordance with title 18, United States Code (which fines shall be paid into the general fund of the Treasury, miscellaneous receipts (pursuant to section 3302 of title 31, United States Code), notwithstanding any other law), or imprisoned not more than 5 years, or both.

[Effective Date]

SEC. 13. EFFECTIVE DATE

This Act shall take effect—

    (1) with respect to a State that on the date of enactment of this Act has a provision in the constitution of the State that would preclude compliance with this Act unless the State maintained separate Federal and State official lists of eligible voters, on the later of—

        (A) January 1, 1996; or

        (B) the date that is 120 days after the date by which, under the constitution of the State as in effect on the date of enactment of this Act, it would be legally possible to adopt and place into effect any amendments to the constitution of the State that are necessary to permit such compliance with this Act without requiring a special election; and

    (2) with respect to any State not described in paragraph (1), on January 1, 1995.

Approved May 20, 1993.

B. WHO DRAFTS A STATUTE?

While a bill (a legislative proposal) often has a single author, a statute usually has many, each of whom has initial views on the subject somewhat different from those of the original bill drafter. To be enacted in a representative democracy, a bill must be supported by a majority of each legislative house and by the executive, or, in the case of an executive veto, by a greater than simple (super) majority in each legislative house. Gaining such support most often requires compromises on particular points with legislators or other interested parties. These compromises among the interested parties are frequently effected through the acceptance of language in bill draft form. Language may be supplied by legislators, legislative staff, representatives of the executive branch, lobbyists, and, where they exist, professional bill drafting services. An example of a bill drafting service is the Office of the Legislative Counsel of the House of Representatives. Its purpose is to "advise and assist the House of Representatives, and its committees and Members, in the achievement of a clear, faithful, and coherent expression of legislative policies." 2 U.S.C. §281a. Its function is to provide technical drafting support, on a nonpartisan basis, to committees and members of the House of Representatives. Many states have similar services, for example, the New York State legislature has a Bill Drafting Commission. Many of these state commissions publish bill drafting manuals that provide excellent guidance for lawyers and other who wish to draft legislation.

To give you an idea of the participatory nature of the bill drafting process, consider the experience of one of the authors, Professor Lane, when he served as counsel to the New York State Senate Minority. Professor Lane was charged with preparing a bill to provide public transportation in the City of New York for people who were without access to public transportation because of a disability. The initial version of the bill, as drafted by Professor Lane, was then introduced by the minority leader in the Senate. A working group of Democratic senators and staff members, and, to a lesser extent, the New York State Legislative Bill Drafting Commission and several lobbyists for the groups representing these people, then began to thoroughly dissect and examine the bill.

As it made its way through the enactment process, the bill underwent a series of changes. Changes were proposed through critiques of the bill's substance and by submission of newly drafted statutory language, designed to replace or amend the initial draft bill. Those proffering such new statutory language were not only other legislators, but included the office of the Governor's Counsel, the Metropolitan Transportation Authority (the agency in charge of New York City's subways and buses), the City of New York, the Eastern Paralyzed Veterans Association, and various lobbyists representing the elderly. These amendments ranged from simple clarifications to significant substantive changes. Many of the suggested language changes were adopted — some because, in the view of the sponsor, the proposed changes improved the language of the bill, some because they improved the substance of the bill, and some because they improved the likelihood of the bill's passage.

C.   THE CONVENTIONS OF STATUTES

1.   The General Form of a Statute

A statute starts with a designation. In the case of the National Voter Registration Act of 1993 excerpted above, the designation is Public Law No. 103-31. Each two-year term of Congress is identified chronologically, and, similarly, each bill enacted into law during that term is assigned a number that reflects the chronological order in which it has been enacted. The National Voter Registration Act of 1993 is the 31st public law enacted by the 103th Congress (1993-1994). Following the designation is a title, an enacting clause, and the body of the statute.

Within the body of the statute, the modern format (with some ordering differences among commentators) sets forth the following parts in the following order: a short title, any purpose and findings, any definitions, the change in law, details, exceptions to the change, agency mandates, sanctions, severability clauses, and effective dates. Professor Dickerson informs this structure with several guidelines:

1. General provisions normally come before special provisions.
2. More important provisions normally come before less important provisions.
3. More frequently used provisions normally come before less frequently used provisions (i.e., the usual should come before the unusual).
4. Permanent provisions normally come before temporary provisions.
5. Technical "housekeeping" provisions, such as effective date provisions, normally come at the end.

Reed Dickerson, The Fundamentals of Legal Drafting 90 (2d ed. 1986). This is the form basically followed by the National Voter Registration Act of 1993.

2.   Amendatory Statutes

Set forth below are provisions from two statutes. Both are very significant statutes because both reflect great changes in the nation's view of political representation. In this section, again, our focus is not on the policies advanced by these statutes (these are addressed in Chapter Two), but on the methods Congress and other legislatures use to amend statutes. Most of the provisions of the statutes are omitted, although §2 of the statute, which is amended by the second statute, is the core provision of both. The amendment reflects a dramatic story that resulted in statutory assurance that the Voting Rights Act could be applied without regard to the discriminatory intent of the state or local government. For a detailing of this story, see Abner J. Mikva and Eric Lane, Legislative Process ch. 6 (1995), and sources cited therein. In these statutes, we again use bold font and brackets to key descriptive phrases to the narrative that follows the statutes. These descriptive phrases are not part of the statutes. As earlier, we only include those parts of the statutes relevant to the forms of amendment.

THE VOTING RIGHTS ACT OF 1965 _____

[Designation]

Pub. L. No. 89-110
89th Congress

AN ACT

[Title]

To enforce the fifteenth amendment to the Constitution of the United States, and for other purposes.

[Enactment Clause]

Be it enacted by the Senate and House of Representatives of the United States of America in Congress assembled,
That this Act shall be known as the

[Short Title]

"Voting Rights Act of 1965." . . .

[The Changes in Law]

SEC. 2. No voting qualification or prerequisite to voting, or standard, practice, or procedure shall be imposed or applied by any State or political subdivision to deny or abridge the right of any citizen of the United States to vote on account of race or color.

SEC. 3. (a) Whenever the Attorney General institutes a proceeding under any statute to enforce the guarantees of the fifteenth amendment in any State or political subdivision the court shall authorize the appointment of Federal examiners by the United States Civil Service Commission in accordance with section 6 to serve for such period of time and for such political subdivisions as the court shall determine is appropriate to enforce the guarantees of the fifteenth amendment (1) as part of any interlocutory order if the court determines that the appointment of such examiners is necessary to enforce such guarantees or (2) as part of any final judgment if the court finds that violations of the fifteenth amendment justifying equitable relief have occurred in such State or subdivision: *Provided*, That the court need not authorize the appointment of examiners if any incidents of denial or abridgement of the right to vote on account of race or color (1) have been few in number and have been promptly and effectively corrected by State or local action, (2) the continuing effect of such incidents has been eliminated, and (3) there is no reasonable probability of their recurrence in the future.

(b) If in a proceeding instituted by the Attorney General under any statute to enforce the guarantees of the fifteenth amendment in any State or political subdivision the court finds that a test or device has been used for the purpose or with the effect of denying or abridging the right of any citizen of the United States to vote on account of race or color, it shall suspend the use of tests and devices in such State or political subdivisions as the court shall determine is appropriate and for such period as it deems necessary. . . .

SEC. 4. (a) To assure that the right of citizens of the United States to vote is not denied or abridged on account of race or color, no citizen shall be denied the right to vote in any Federal, State, or local election because of his failure to comply with any test or device in any State with respect to which the determinations have been made under subsection (b) or in any political subdivision with respect to which such determinations have been made as a separate unit, unless the United States District Court for the District of Columbia in an action for a declaratory judgment brought by such State or subdivision against the United States has determined that no such test or device has been used during the five years preceding the filing of the action for the purpose or with the effect of denying or abridging the right to vote on account of race or color: *Provided*, That no such declaratory judgment shall issue with respect to any plaintiff for a period of five years after the entry of a final judgment of any court of the United States, other than the denial of a declaratory judgment under this section, whether entered prior to or after the enactment of this Act, determining that denials or abridgments of the right to vote on account of race or color through the use of such tests or devices have occurred anywhere in the territory of such plaintiff.

An action pursuant to this subsection shall be heard and determined by a court of three judges in accordance with the provisions of section 2284 of title 28 of the United States Code and any appeal shall lie to the Supreme Court. The court shall retain jurisdiction of any action pursuant to this subsection for five years after judgment and shall reopen the action upon motion of the Attorney General alleging that a test or device has been used for the purpose or with the effect of denying or abridging the right to vote on account of race or color.

If the Attorney General determines that he has no reason to believe that any such test or device has been used during the five years preceding the filing of the action for the purpose or with the effect of denying or abridging the right to vote on account of race or color he shall consent to the entry of such judgment. . . .

VOTING RIGHTS AMENDMENTS OF 1982

[Designation]

Pub. L. No. 97-205
97th Congress

AN ACT

[Title]

To amend the Voting Rights Act of 1965 to extend the effect of certain provisions, and for other purposes.

[Enactment Clause]

Be it enacted by the Senate and House of Representatives of the United States of America in Congress assembled,
That this act may be cited as the

[Short Title]

"Voting Rights Act Amendments of 1982." . . .

[Amendment by Reference]

SEC. 2. (a) Subsection (a) of section 4 of the Voting Rights Act of 1965 is amended by striking out "seventeen years" each place it appears and inserting in lieu thereof "nineteen years."

(b) Effective on and after August 5, 1984, subsection (a) of section 4 of the Voting Rights Act of 1965 is amended—

(1) by inserting "(1)" after "(a)";

(2) by inserting "or in any political subdivision of such State (as such subdivision existed on the date such determinations were made with respect to such State), though such determinations were not made with respect to such subdivision as a separate unit," before "or in any political subdivision with respect to which" each place it appears;

(3) by striking out "in an action for a declaratory judgment" the first place it appears and all that follows through "color through the use of such tests or devices have occurred anywhere in the territory of such plaintiff.", and inserting in lieu thereof "issues a declaratory judgment under this section."; . . .

[Amendment by Reenactment]

SEC. 3. Section 2 of the Voting Rights Act of 1965 is amended to read as follows:

"SEC. 2. (a) No voting qualifications or prerequisite to voting or standard, practice, or procedure shall be imposed or applied by any State or political subdivision in a manner which results in a denial or abridgement of the right of any citizen of the United States to vote on account of race or color, or in contravention of the guarantees set forth in section 4(f)(2), as provided in subsection (b).

(b) A violation of subsection (a) is established if, based on the totality of circumstances, it is shown that the political processes leading to nomination or election in the State or political subdivision are not equally open to participation by members of a class of citizens protected by subsection (a) in that its members have less opportunity than other members of the electorate to participate in the political process and to elect representatives of their choice. The extent to which members of a protected class have been elected to office in the State or political subdivision is one circumstance which may be considered:

Provided, That nothing in this section establishes a right to have members of a protected class elected in numbers equal to their proportion in the population." . . .

Approved June 29, 1992.

The Voting Rights Act of 1965 is freestanding or new. This does not mean that the subject matter of this statute has not been the subject matter of prior law, but that this statute does not expressly amend existing statutes. It may, however, implicitly amend or repeal provisions of existing statutes if those existing provisions conflict with its provisions.

The second statute is, by its terms, an amendment to existing law. It contains two separate approaches to amendment. The first is exemplified by §2 of the Voting Rights Amendments of 1982, which is an *amendment by reference.* As reading §2 of the Voting Rights Amendments of 1982 demonstrates, this approach is extremely hard to follow, both for legislators trying to follow the process and for the public trying to understand the law. Without a side-by-side comparison between the amendment and the provision of law being amended, the reader cannot understand the effects of the amendment.

The second approach to statutory amendment is exemplified by §3 of the Amendments. This is an *amendment by reenactment* or *restatement.* As you can tell, it is much easier to follow, as it shows all of the changes to §2 of the Voting Rights Act of 1965. Because of this ease in comprehension, most state constitutions require the reenactment-restatement method. Using this form, "a citizen or legislator [will] not be required to search out other statutes which are amended to know the law on the subject treated in the new statute." Washington Education Association v. State, 604 P.2d 950, 952 (Wash. 1980). For example, Article 4, §9 of the California Constitution provides: "A statute may not be amended by reference to its title. A section of a statute may not be amended unless the section is reenacted as amended."

One disadvantage to this approach is that it does not show what has been changed without comparison with the provision that has been amended. To resolve this problem many jurisdictions strike out the text being omitted and redline or underscore the text being added. Following this model, a sample excerpt of the 1982 amendment to §2 of the Voting Rights Act of 1965 would be reflected in the statute as follows (we use underscoring in place of redlining in this example):

> SEC. 1. Sec. 2. of the Voting Rights Act of 1965 is amended as follows:
> "SEC. 2. No voting qualification or prerequisite to voting, or standard, practice, or procedure shall be imposed or applied by any State or political subdivision ~~to deny or abridge~~ <u>in a manner which results in a denial or abridgement of</u> the right of any citizen of the United States to vote on account of race or color. . . . "

3.   The Title of a Statute

Every statute has an official title. This is customary for all federal statutes except for the titles of appropriation bills, which are statutorily required. 1 U.S.C. §105 (1988). In most states, titles are required by constitution. In some states, such as New York, titles are required only by legislative rule. The titles of the three statutes set forth above are "An Act to establish national voter registration procedures for Federal elections, and for other purposes"; "An Act to enforce the fifteenth amendment to the Constitution of the United States, and for other purposes"; and "An Act to amend the Voting Rights Act of 1965 to extend the effect of certain provisions, and for other purposes." These titles, known as long titles, are descriptive in that they attempt to describe the statute's purpose. For purposes of easier reference, legislatures sometimes, as part of the act itself, give statutes short titles. Each of these statutes (but not all statutes) has a short title: "The National Voter Registration Act of 1993," "The Voting Rights Act of 1965," and "The Voting Rights Act Amendments of 1982." In legislative practice, titles provide notice to legislators and to the public of the substance of pending legislation. It is the bill title that usually appears on the agendas for legislative committee meetings and legislative floor action. For this reason titles ought to be informative.

Modern authorities on bill drafting assert that — excluding titles so general as to be meaningless — the best title is one which is brief and kept in general terms, not one which is an abstract of all the incidental provisions of the bill. If the title expresses the general object or purpose of the bill, all matters fairly and reasonably connected therewith and all measures which will or may facilitate the accomplishment of such object or purpose are properly incorporated into the act and are germane to the title.

New York State Legislative Bill Drafting Commission, Bill Drafting Manual 12 (n.d.).

Consider similarly the following title for an omnibus tax bill from New York. (This is just the first of three pages.)

CHAPTER 57 OF THE LAWS OF 1992

AN ACT to amend the tax law, in relation to retaining in 1993 the state personal income tax rates and standard deduction amounts in effect during the 1992 tax year and providing for the personal income tax rates, household credit and standard deduction amounts for tax years beginning after 1993; to amend article 30 of the tax law and chapter 17 of title 11 of the administrative code of the city of New York, in relation to retaining in 1993 the tax rate tables, household credit and standard deduction amounts in effect in the 1992 tax year and providing for tax rate tables, household credit and standard deduction amounts for tax years beginning after 1993 under the New York city personal income tax on residents; to repeal section 18 of chapter 55 of the laws of 1992 amending the tax law and other laws relating to taxes, in relation to withholding; to amend the tax law, in relation to extending certain business surcharge taxes and the current rate applicable to the minimum taxable income base under article 9-A thereof; to amend the tax law, in relation to the rate adjustment calculations under the petroleum business tax imposed by article 13-A thereof and to the disposition of revenues therefrom; to amend the tax law, in relation to the estimated provisions of the state franchise and certain business taxes, to conform to estimated tax provisions recently enacted for federal purposes; to amend the tax law, in relation to increasing the rates of taxes on cigarettes and tobacco products imposed by article 20 of such law; to amend the tax law, in relation to the deposit and disposition of certain revenues in the metropolitan mass transportation operating assistance fund and the general fund and repealing certain provisions upon expiration thereof; to amend the vehicle and traffic law, in relation to reducing regional design plate fees; to amend the tax law, in relation to amending the definition of consideration and original purchase price and restructuring certain penalties imposed with respect to the tax on gains derived from certain real property transfers; the uncoupling from certain federal income tax provisions in the calculation of the franchise tax on entire net income of insurance corporations; to amend the abandoned property law, in relation to security deposits held by title insurers and agents; to amend chapter 41 of the laws of 1990, relating to authorizing and directing the transfer of hazardous waste remedial fund industry fee transfer account balances and receipts to the general fund and the state finance law, in relation to industry fee surcharges and the calculations relating thereto; to amend the state finance law, in relation to the establishment of a New York state passenger facility charge fund; . . .

As noted earlier, in many states, titles are the subject of constitutional or statutory provisions. The formalization of title requirements is related to a decline in the reading of bills to the assembled legislative body. Historically, because of the high rate of illiteracy, each bill, in almost every legislative body, was read three times by the clerk before a vote was taken. Usually these readings had to be accomplished on different days. As this practice changed because of growing legislative literacy and growing legislative agendas, the importance of titles as notice of the subject matter of bills began to grow. It was through the title that legislators and other interested parties learned of the bill's subject and determined whether they ought to read it. On this basis the accuracy of titles became significant. "Otherwise a harmless-looking title may cover a vicious bill; it may be made the sheep's clothing for a legislative wolf." Charles L. Jones, Statute Law Making in the United States 64 (1912). For a complete listing of information on title requirements, see Inside the Legislative Process 52-53 (National Conference of State Legislators, 1991).

Title requirements have had considerable costs associated with them. Mainly they have given rise to considerable litigation that has sometimes resulted in otherwise valid legislation being declared unconstitutional. This has caused a number of states to revisit their title requirements. Illinois, for example, amended its Constitution in 1970 to eliminate title requirements. In 1986, Texas amended its Constitution to provide (in amendatory form):

ART. 3, Sec 35. (a) No bill . . . shall contain more than one subject, which shall be expressed in its title. But if any subject shall be embraced in any act, which shall not be expressed in the title, such act shall be void only as to so much thereof, as shall not be so expressed.

(b) The rules of procedure of each house shall require that the subject of each bill be expressed in its title in a manner that gives the legislature and the public reasonable notice of that subject. The legislature is solely responsible for determining compliance with the rule.

(c) A law, including a law enacted before the effective date of this subsection, may not be held void on the basis of an insufficient title.

Titles are often used as a basis to refer bills to appropriate legislative committees. As the assignment of the bill to a committee may be the most important decision over the fate of the bill (see Chapter 3), titles are sometimes written in a manner calculated to assure that a favorable committee (in situations in which alternatives are possible) will consider the bill. A good example of this is provided by one of the authors, Judge Mikva. He recalls that while he was serving in Congress in 1969, he was told about the existence of a detention camp located in the United States and intended for "subversives." This camp had been established pursuant to the Emergency Detention Act of 1950. Concerned about the continuation of the policies expressed in this act, Mikva attempted to repeal the legislation. He discovered that a group of Japanese Americans was similarly attempting a repeal, reflecting the experience of the internment camps during World War II. See Korematsu v. United States, 323 U.S. 214 (1944). Unfortunately, the bill promoted by the Japanese Americans had been languishing in the House Committee on Internal Security, an unfriendly committee. It was sent there as a result of its title: "A bill to repeal the Emergency Detention Act of 1950." As part of the strategy, which finally led to the repeal of this 1950 statute, the bill was reintroduced with a new title: "A bill to amend title 18, United States Code, to prohibit the establishment of emergency detention camps. . . . " This bill was sent to the Judiciary Committee, a sympathetic committee, which had jurisdiction over title 18 amendments. The bill was favorably reported to the House and later became law.

One final word on titles. Recall that they come *before* the enactment clause. They are not part of the body of the statute. This can be significant when interpretating statutes. See, for example, Church of the Holy Trinity v. United States, 143 U.S. 457 (1892).

4.   The Enacting Clause

The statute's title precedes an enacting clause that reads, in the case of the excerpted statutes above, "Be it enacted by the Senate and House of Representatives of the United States of America in Congress assembled." The purpose of an enacting clause is to provide formal notice that what follows is uniquely important. It also serves to distinguish a bill from other forms of legislative communications, such as resolutions. (Resolutions, except in certain cases when signed by the president, are communications that deal with matters within the prerogative of one or both houses. They do not have the force of law.) The federal enacting clause is prescribed by statute, 1 U.S.C. §101. State enacting clauses are frequently prescribed by constitutional provisions. For example, Article IV, §8, of the Illinois Constitution provides that: "[t]he enacting clause of this State shall be: "Be it enacted by the People of the State of Illinois, represented in the General Assembly." The enacting clause provision is usually considered mandatory, and its absence (a rare occurrence) invalidates a statute. See, e.g., People v. Dettenthaler, 77 N.W. 450 (Mich. 1898).

5.   The Number of Subjects in a Statute

Statutes may contain a variety of distinct subjects. Such legislation is known as *omnibus legislation*. Its goal is generally to forge support for each subject of the legislation by tying the many subjects together. In other words, a legislator will support the omnibus bill because he or she supports some part of it. This practice is sometimes referred to as *logrolling*, but logrolling is a broader practice that more traditionally includes the promise of one legislator (A) to support the legislation of a second legislator (B) in return for legislator B's promise to support the legislation of legislator A. Omnibus legislation is also used to provide a shield to legislators by allowing them to argue that they supported unpopular provisions of a bill in order to enact popular provisions. Such legislation is occasionally used to force executive approval of disfavored legislation by combining it with legislation favored by the executive. This leaves the executive with an all-or-nothing choice in the decision of whether to exercise the veto and accounts for the inclusion of the line item veto in some state constitutions.

Over 40 states have constitutional requirements known as *single subject rules*, which restrict statutes to single subjects. Typical of a single subject rule is Article 4, §8 of the California Constitution: "A statute shall embrace but one subject. . . . " The primary purpose of single subject restrictions is to prohibit logrolling. Single subject rules, a least in theory, also help create a more orderly legislative process by focusing legislative attention on a single issue and avoiding the detractions caused by the introduction of nongermane subjects. For a classical study of single subject rules, see Millard H. Rudd, No Law Shall Embrace More Than One Subject, 42 Minn. L. Rev. 389 (1958). It is questionable whether the single subject rule accomplishes its purposes. Certainly it does not restrict vote trading on separate bills. Moreover, the definition of a single subject is elusive. The New York tax bill noted on pages 159-160 may cover a single subject (taxes) or several subjects (a number of taxes).

Consider the following problem. During his tenure as a member of the Illinois State Legislature, Judge Mikva encountered a bill that had as its subject the creation of a number of commissions. Assume the bill's title read: "A bill for the establishment of certain commissions." Among the commissions listed in the bill was a Fair Employment Practices Commission that Mikva had proposed and also several that Mikva opposed. Illinois has a single subject rule. Article 4, §8 of the Illinois Constitution provides that: "[b]ills, except for appropriations and for the codification, revision or rearrangement of laws, shall be confined to one subject." Off and on during his tenure, Mikva had used this provision to argue in opposition to legislation that had been cobbled together by the legislative leadership. He wanted to be loyal to this position, but in the end, supported the legislation, consoling himself that the bill's subject was singularly "commissions."

The problem above illustrates a tension that sometimes occurs between the imperatives of the legislative process—enacting laws—and those of externally imposed rules of legislative procedure. While Mikva was a supporter of the single subject rule, much of his opposition to earlier omnibus legislation had been based on the merits of the legislation he opposed, rather than on the bill's form. Being confronted with legislation that contained provisions important to him raised a different question that made him read the rule as broadly as possible. Except in extreme cases, courts have not compelled narrower readings. There has been a uniform and principled reluctance on the part of courts throughout the country to overturn statutes on such a basis. For a detailed exploration of these points, see Millard H. Rudd, No Law Shall Embrace More Than One Subject, 42 Minn. L. Rev. 389 (1958).

6. Statutory Findings and Statements of Purpose

Sometimes statutes provide details about the concerns that led to their enactment. An earlier example of such a section is the purpose clause of the Americans with Disabilities Act of 1990, found in Chapter One, pages 8 to 9. Section 2 of the National Voter Registration Act of 1993 also contains such a legislative finding. The example below is excerpted from a New York statute, the New York City Municipal Water Finance Authority Act.

SEC. 1. LEGISLATIVE FINDINGS AND DECLARATION OF PURPOSES

It is hereby found and declared that the maintenance of the water supply systems and the development of new sources of supply in and for the city of New York . . . are required to enhance the achievement of statewide goals of protecting public health, promoting conservation of scarce natural resources and stimulating economic growth. . . .

It is further found that alternative financing methods which, according to the provisions of the state constitution, must be approved by the Legislature, can be used to directly

provide the capital necessary to maintain the city's water and
sewer systems in adequate condition so that they continue to
provide vital water and sewer services to the public. . . .

It is further found that one such alternative method, the issuance of municipal securities secured by local user fees for the
use or services of any self-sufficient water and sewage system,
or other revenues, has been favorably received by investors
even during periods when market conditions restrict the sale of
municipal general obligations. . . . The problems of the cost and
availability of capital make necessary the creation of a new sin-
gle-purpose entity to assist such city in financing water and
sewer system improvements through the issuance of such securities.

N.Y. Pub. Auth. Law §§1045-a–1046, 1984 N.Y. Laws chs. 513-
515.

Such sections serve to provide the public with the broad
reasoning behind the enactment of the legislation and statutory interpreters with a context in which the more detailed language of the statute, particularly if it is ambiguous, can be
applied. One example of this latter use is the applicability of
the above New York provision in a case testing the legality of
the New York Water Finance Authority's financing of the New
York Water Board's proposed purchase of the New York City
water system by a New York State agency.

To the extent that it can be argued that the meaning of the word
"water project" generally and/or as set forth in section 1045-I is
ambiguous, the term must be interpreted in a manner which is
consistent with the purposes of the statute. The purpose of the
Water Finance Act was to facilitate the financing of water and
sewerage repairs and improvements. This is clear from section 1
of the Act . . . which sets forth the Legislative Findings and Declaration of Purpose.

Giuliani v. Hevesi, unpublished op., Mar. 13, 1996 (Solomon,
J.). On the federal level, purposes and findings clauses have a
unique purpose. "Courts frequently do give weight to legislative findings when construing regulatory laws and other laws
affecting commerce in cases where the constitutional basis for
the Federal actions may be open to question." Lawrence E.
Filson, The Legislative Drafter's Desk Reference 120 (1992).

7.   Definitions

Statutes frequently contain definitions such as the ones in
§3 of the National Voter Registration Act of 1993. Through
definitions, a legislative body can give a word or phrase any
meaning it chooses. Definitions are used in a statute to limit
the common meaning of certain words or phrases, or to make
sure that certain words and phrases are given a particular
meaning. The addition of a definition section to a statute may
be only a matter of purposely clear drafting (the use of the
term "election" in the National Registration Act of 1993 or the
use of the term "test or device" in the Voting Rights Act of
1965), but it also may be the result of legislative compromises
(such as defining employers as those who employ more than
25 persons in the Civil Rights Act of 1964) or a desire to limit
the discretion of administrative agencies or the courts. In fact,
after statutory sanctions, statutory definitions can be the most
important part of a statute.

In contrast, common language in statutes should not be
statutorily defined. "A term that is familiar, clear, and used in
its dictionary sense should never be formally defined (unless
there are special circumstances that call for reassurance to the
reader) — it would be unnecessary and might create doubts
about the meaning of other familiar words in the bill."
Lawrence E. Filson, The Legislative Drafter's Desk Reference
120 (1992).

8.   Remedies and Sanctions

Statutes often contain remedies and sanctions, allowing
the government and private individuals to bring lawsuits and
authorizing or requiring imprisonment, fines, damages, and
injunctions for statutory violations. These are among the most
important provisions in a statute and are frequently the focus
of legislative debate. For example, who would have opposed
the Voting Rights Act of 1965 if it had simply provided that
"no voting qualification . . . shall be imposed or applied . . . by
any state . . . to deny or abridge the right of any citizen . . . to
vote on account of race or color"? The inclusion of provisions

permitting federal enforcement of the act's provisions was one of the major points of debate.

9.   Severability Clauses

Section 19 of the Voting Rights Act of 1965 is a *severability clause*. It provides:

> SEC. 19. If any provision of this Act or the application thereof to any person or circumstances is held invalid, the remainder of the Act and application of the provision to other persons not similarly situated or to other circumstances shall not be affected thereby.

Almost all statutes include such clauses, although the National Voters Registration Act of 1993 does not contain one. Severability clauses make clear to the courts that it is the legislative intent to preserve as much of the statute as possible in case part of it is invalidated.

In some instances, a better approach to statutory drafting is to include an *inseverability clause*, which specifically ties certain provisions together. If one of these provisions is invalidated by the courts, the other provisions would also be invalidated by statutory command. Inseverability clauses protect important legislative compromises from being undermined. An example of such a clause is found in a bill proposing an amendment to the Federal Election Campaign Act Amendments of 1974. The bill failed to pass the House. It provided:

EFFECT OF INVALIDITY ON OTHER PROVISIONS OF ACT

> If section 501, 502, or 503 of title V of FECA (as added by this section), or any part thereof, is held to be invalid, all provisions of, and amendments made by, this Act shall be treated as invalid.

Judge Mikva, when in Congress, explored the use of an inseverability clause as a remedy for the problem created by the decision in Immigration and Naturalization Service v. Chadha, 462 U.S. 919 (1983). In *Chadha*, the Court struck down Congress's power to veto a regulation of an administrative

agency, except through the enactment of a statute. As one solution to the problem they saw left by the decision, Mikva and
others considered adding to an agency appropriation bill a
provision containing a right of legislative veto and an inseverability clause. For example, added to an appropriation bill for
purchase of parkland would be a congressional right to veto
the locations. These would be tied together by an inseverability
clause that would invalidate the appropriation if the veto provision was successfully challenged. In the end, the approach
was abandoned for various political and policy reasons.

10. *The Effective Date of a Statute*

Among the most important provisions of any statute is its
effective date. For the legislator, choosing an effective date
raises two questions: When should the statute go into effect?
What does *go into effect* mean? The National Voter Registration
Act of 1993 contains several effective dates; the Voting Rights
Act of 1965 contains none. The Voting Rights Amendment of
1982 provides that it should take effect "immediately." What is
the effective date of the Voting Rights Act of 1965? Under
federal law, statutes that contain no effective date become
effective on the date they become law, that is, signed by the
president, enacted over the president's veto, or, in the absence
of presidential action, pursuant to Article I, §7 of the U.S.
Constitution. See 2 U.S.C. §106a.

Many state constitutions and statutes regulate the effective
dates of statutes. Article 4, §7 of the California Constitution
provides that: "a statute enacted at a regular session shall go
into effect on January 1 next following a 90-day period from
the date of enactment of the statute." This provision also provides for certain exceptions to this rule. A more flexible version
is found in the Illinois Constitution:

> The General Assembly shall provide by law for a uniform effec-
> tive date for laws passed prior to July 1 of a calendar year. The
> General Assembly may provide for a different effective date in
> any law passed prior to July 1. A bill passed after June 30 shall
> not become effective prior to July 1 of the next calendar year un-
> less the General Assembly by the vote of three-fifths of the

members elected to each house provides for an earlier effective date.

Ill. Const. art. 4, §10. The different treatment of bills passed before July 1 and bills passed after June 30 is intended to encourage the state legislature to finish its business before the end of June unless there are special problems to consider. Section 43 of the Legislative Law of New York (McKinney's 1991) provides that "[e]very law unless a different time shall be described therein shall take effect on the twentieth day after it shall have become law."

Sometimes statutory provisions setting forth the effective date of a statute do not inform as to the timing of the statute's applicability. For example, the Civil Rights Act of 1991 provides that its provision should take effect immediately, but, as discussed below, questions remain as to whether it should be applied to discriminatory actions that took place before its enactment (retroactively) or only to such acts that occur after its enactment (prospectively). Statutes, except for those establishing crimes, may be applied retroactively, and whether they are or are not depends on the language of the statute and its interpretation.

The choice of an effective date for a statute is frequently one of the most hotly contested points in the consideration of a piece of legislation. Consider the following example provided by Judge Mikva, from his days as a member of the Illinois legislature. A child had fallen through the rotted railing of a common stairway on the third floor of an apartment building and had died. Under the terms of the lease, the tenant had waived liability for the landlord's negligence. Such lease provisions were strictly enforced under Illinois law. Mikva introduced a bill declaring such lease provisions to be against public policy. For his effective date he wanted the statute to apply to all existing leases and to all claims then pending or that thereafter may arise under existing or prior existing leases, except as otherwise barred by any statute of limitations. Mikva wanted to cover every accident, not yet subject to a final judgment, except if it were too late to commence the action because of the statute of limitations. That would also mean that if a claim had been appealed and was before the Illinois Supreme Court, the court would apply the new statute.

While a great many supported the bill's policy goal, Mikva's effective date caused considerable dispute. Some argued for covering existing leases, but only for accidents that occurred after the date the statute was enacted, while others argued for covering only new leases. In the end, to gain enough support to pass the bill, Mikva accepted a compromise that obscured the bill's effective date. It definitely did not cover the accident that led to the introduction of the legislation, but whether it applied to accidents that already had occurred but had not yet been fully litigated was left to the courts to decide.

Such disputes over the effective date of a statute are not easily resolved. Consider the Civil Rights Act of 1991. This bill was intended to resolve problems created by several Supreme Court decisions that Congress believed had too severely restricted the reach of Title VII (Employment Discrimination) of the Civil Rights Act of 1964. Among the major issues was the effective date. This was of particular import because the bill contained new provisions on compensatory and punitive damages.

One group of the bill's supporters, led in the Senate by Senator Kennedy, wanted the bill to apply retroactively to cover discriminatory actions that predated the enactment date of the statute. Another group, led by Senators Dansforth and Dole, argued for prospective application only covering discriminatory actions that postdated the statute. This was a make-or-break issue for each group, and the failure to resolve it might have led to legislative inaction or the defeat of any bill. As a compromise, §402 of this statute provides that "this Act and the amendments made by this Act shall take effect upon enactment."

Who prevailed in this dispute? The Supreme Court resolved this dispute in favor of prospectivity. In Landgraf v. USI Film Products, 511 U.S. 244 (1994), the Court decided that there is a presumption in favor of the prospective application of a statute unless Congress has clearly expressed a contrary (retroactive) intent.

D.   PRIVATE AND LOCAL STATUTES

Statutes are not always of a general nature. Sometimes they address the interests of an individual or a small group of people. These are known as *private statutes* or, in most states when such legislation is directed toward a particular locality within the state, as *local statutes*. The legislative granting of corporate charters or franchises, now mostly prohibited, are examples of private statutes. Similarly, Congress's enactment of laws that allow named individuals to immigrate to the United States or enjoin the deportation of particular individuals are private statutes. Congress and state legislatures also enact private legislation to resolve various types of individual claims. Such statutes may include waiving a statute of limitations for a particular individual, waiving the requirement of refunds for an unauthorized payment of funds for services actually performed, or awarding damages in tort claims. In this last group, Congress has voted for settlements in several cases flowing from the government's experiments involving hallucinogenic drugs during the 1950s.

There is an equity impulse behind most private legislation. The usual situation is a unique problem for which no other institution can or will provide a remedy. Consider the following New York bill that was introduced after a particular governmental agency decision had been upheld by New York State's highest court. See In re O'Rourke v. Kirby, 54 N.Y.2d 8 (1981).

STATE OF NEW YORK

S. 7691   A. 9475

SENATE — ASSEMBLY

January 20, 1982

AN ACT in relation to requiring the Suffolk county department of social services to return one Stephanie Petzold, a six and one-half year old child, to her former foster parent, Mrs. Veronica O'Rourke, and to direct such department to permit the adoption of Stephanie Petzold by Mrs. O'Rourke.

The People of the State of New York, represented in Senate and Assembly, do enact as follows:

SECTION 1.   The legislature hereby finds and declares that Stephanie Petzold is a six and one-half year old child who has been removed from the only home and mother figure she has ever known and been placed by the Suffolk county department of social services with a total stranger, perhaps only to be returned to the "limbo" of foster care again. Stephanie's natural mother is deceased and her natural father unknown, not being named on her birth certificate nor ever attempting to contact Stephanie.

The recommended time period established by the legislature for placement of a child with a foster parent, in this case Mrs. Veronica O'Rourke of 36 Wooded Way, Calverton, New York, has been recently reduced from two years to eighteen months in recognition of the fact that prolonged care and custody by a foster parent gives rise to a presumption that the "best interest" of the child is served by remaining with the foster parent. Suffolk county department of social services has allowed Stephanie to remain with Mrs. O'Rourke for six consecutive years.

Mrs. O'Rourke has claimed that Stephanie will experience permanent psychological harm if she is removed from her custody and she has shown, through expert testimony, that Stephanie identifies with her as "psychological parent." Stephanie deserves and requires stability of continuity in parenting.

§2.   Notwithstanding the provisions of any law, rule, regulation or order to the contrary, the legislature hereby directs the Suffolk county department of social services to return Stephanie Petzold to the care and custody of Mrs. Veronica O'Rourke, her former foster parent of more than six years and residing at 36 Wooded Way, Calverton, New York, and to supply any necessary assistance to lessen any disorientation which Stephanie may experience, and to assist both Miss Petzold and Mrs. O'Rourke in compensating for any physical or emotional problem from which Stephanie may suffer.

§3.   The Suffolk county department of social services is hereby directed to allow Mrs. Veronica O'Rourke, upon proper application under article seven of the domestic relations law, to adopt Stephanie Petzold as her child.

§4.   This act shall take effect immediately.

This bill passed the New York State Assembly and was sent to the Senate, where many senators supported it. It did not become law. During the period between introduction and adoption in the Assembly, a large majority of senators began to question the wisdom of such an act and finally stopped its passage. A broader bill, allowing for foster parents to adopt foster children in certain circumstances, was ultimately enacted.

A state's authority to enact such private legislation is found in its plenary legislative power, although, in many states, such power has been restricted to prohibit certain types of private bills. For Congress, such bills must fall within the scope of one of its enumerated powers.

In many jurisdictions, private and local bills are treated differently from general legislation. In Congress, for example, there is separate consideration of this type of legislation on fixed days during the month.

CHAPTER FIVE

The Publication of Statutes

In this chapter, we offer an introduction to an important subject, the publication of statutes, about which few students of law have any systematic knowledge. The nation's federal and state constitutions require written vehicles for the introduction and enactment of laws. Bills and statutes are written to provide notice to the legislative members of the exact matters under legislative consideration and, after enactment, to give clear and accessible notice to the public of the law. But the enactment of a written statute alone does not constitute notice. For this end, a statute must be published.

For most law students and attorneys, statutes are the sequentially numbered provisions published in the various titles of the United States Code Annotated and various annotated state codes, for example, McKinney's Consolidated Laws of New York Annotated, Smith-Hurd Illinois Annotated Statutes, and West's Annotated California Code. But codes are not the only place that statutes are published, and in most cases, for reasons discussed in section E of this chapter, they do not constitute official publications of the law and are not, consequently, conclusive evidence of the law. The provisions of most codes constitute only prima facie evidence of the law. Conclusive evidence of the law, on the federal level and in most states, is the law in the form it is enacted, known as an *enrolled bill*. The issue of statutory evidence is discussed in section C of this chapter.

A.   ENROLLED BILLS

An *enrolled bill* is one that has passed both houses of a legislative body (except in Nebraska, which, like local legislatures, has one house) in identical form. The bill, is then presented to the president or governor. The enrolling process, presided over by the enrolling clerk of the house in which the bill originated, is intended to make sure that the bill presented to the executive is a bill that has passed the houses of the legislature in identical form.

In Congress, as in most state processes, enrolling entails superimposing on the bill that first passed the originating house any subsequent amendments that both legislative houses have adopted. For example, assume that a bill passes the House of Representatives. This bill, signed by the Clerk of the House as having passed the House on a particular date (known then as an *engrossed bill*), is sent to the Senate. Assume that, in the Senate, amendment 1 and amendment 2 to the House bill are adopted. At this point, neither house has passed an identical bill. The bill with the two amendments, signed by the Secretary of the Senate, is then sent back to the House of Representatives. In the House, amendment 1 is adopted, but amendment 2 is not. Neither house has yet passed identical bills. The two versions of the bill (the Senate version with amendments 1 and 2, the House version with amendment 1) are now sent to a conference committee in an attempt to resolve the dispute. (The conference committee is selected by the House Speaker and the presiding officer of the Senate. Conferees are usually members of the substantive committee that reported the legislation and are recommended by the committee chair and ranking minority member. See Chapter Three, section C12.) The conference committee reports a compromise on amendment 2, as set forth in a conference report. That compromise is sent to both houses; if both houses adopt the compromise (known as a *conference report*), identical bills have been enacted. At this point, it is the task of the House enrolling clerk (because the bill originated in the House) to take the bill that first passed the House (the engrossed bill) and add to it amendment 1 and the compromised amendment 2. This enrolled bill is then printed, in Congress on parchment paper, signed by the presiding officer of each house (the Speaker of the House of Representatives, the President Pro Tem of the Senate, or other designated representatives or senators), and then presented to the president.

The enrolled bill evidences the legislative enactment, and in most cases is conclusive evidence of the law. The president (but see discussion on page 140) and the governors of some states are allowed to veto items in an appropriation bill. (In Washington, parts of a nonappropriation bill may also be vetoed.) In cases in which an item veto is exercised, the remainder (the nonvetoed portion) of the bill becomes law. The enrolled bill, then, is the bill approved by the governor, which is different from the bill first presented to him or her.

B. SLIP LAWS

An enrolled federal bill that becomes law, either by executive action (signature), by executive inaction (pocket approval), or by legislative override of an executive veto, is sent by the executive or, in the case of enactment by override, by the appropriate legislative official to the Archives of the United States, where the original is officially stored pursuant to 1 U.S.C. §106a. Most states require that enrolled bills be filed with their secretary of state. For example, New Jersey requires that enacted (enrolled) bills be delivered

> to the Secretary of State, to be filed in his office, in such order that the laws . . . of each sitting of the Legislature shall be kept separately, according to the year in which they shall be passed, and not delivered to any person whatsoever, but safely kept by the Secretary of State in his office, and not suffered to be taken or removed therefrom on any pretext whatsoever.

N.J. Stat. Ann. §1:2-5 (West 1992). Enrolled bills are generally not accessible, and few legislators or staff members have ever seen one.

The first official publication of a new federal law is referred to as a *slip law*. The slip law is simply the enrolled bill after it has become law (by executive approval, by executive inaction, or by legislative override of an executive veto). The National Voter Registration Act of 1993, excerpted in Chapter

Four, pages 144-149, is an example of a federal slip law. A slip law contains the text of the new statute, the date of enactment, and (since 1976) a citation to the volume of the Statutes at Large in which it will appear. Federal slip laws also contain marginal notes referring to any statute mentioned in the text, (since 1974) the United States Code classification of the statute or provisions of the statute, and a legislative history of the statute, with references to the Congressional Record. Federal slip laws are prepared by the Office of the Federal Register in the National Archives and Records Administration and are attainable through the Government Printing Office. They are also found in the United States Code Service (ASCUS) advance service, the United States Code Congressional and Administrative News (U.S.C.C.A.N.), and through various electronic services.

State slip laws, sometimes known as *chapter laws* or *pamphlet laws*, are generally less accessible. Some states officially publish copies of individual statutes, but many do not. But in almost all states, private publishers publish copies of newly enacted laws as part of their advance sheets service.

C.   SLIP LAW COLLECTIONS—STATUTES AT LARGE, SESSION LAWS, AND OTHERS

At the end of each legislative session (equal to one year), the slip laws enacted during that session are collected sequentially by public law number or chapter number and published as *session laws*. The collection of federal slip laws is known as the *Statutes at Large*. The Statutes at Large are required to be published at the end of each legislative session of Congress by the Archivist of the United States and to contain "all the laws ... enacted during each regular session of Congress." 1 U.S.C. §112. States have similar publications. For example, §44 of the Legislative Law of New York (McKinney's 1991) requires the annual publication of the session laws, arranged by chapter numbers. Session laws are also unofficially published by private publishers. For a listing of the session law publications in each state, see the latest edition of The Bluebook, A Uniform System of Citation.

D.   CODES

When you are searching for an applicable statute or reading provisions of a statute in a case, an article, or a brief, it is most likely that your reference point will be the United States Code, the United States Code Annotated, one of the 50 state annotated codes, or the codes (annotated or not), of the multitude of national municipalities. Codes are the consolidation and systematic arrangement (*codification*) by subject matter of a particular jurisdiction's statutes. *Annotated* refers to the inclusion of various references to cases interpreting statutory provisions, law review articles discussing the particular statute or provision, and other references or cross-references.

The United States Code is the consolidation and codification of the Statutes at Large or slip laws. Every state has a code, all of which are listed in The Bluebook, A Uniform System of Citation.

The need for codes is evident. They give life to statutory law. The Statutes at Large or similar collections moreover are not useful for determining those laws in force at a given time or applicable to a particular subject. For example, assume you are asked to determine what, if any, federal statutory law is applicable to a decision by a national bank in a rural community to sell insurance to its customers or to strangers. (We use this example because its facts are the basis of the case discussed on page 183.) Assume further that codes do not exist. How would you perform this research? Your most systematic choice would be to start with the first volume of the Statutes at Large and work forward to the most recent volume to find any applicable statute or statutory provision (in the case of omnibus statutes, those that cover more than one subject). You would then check whether that statute or provision had been repealed or amended by later statutes or provisions, until you arrived at what in your view is the present law. Such a task would be overwhelming. Codification solves this problem.

The United States Code contains the public laws of the United States organized by title (topic). The code is prepared and published, pursuant to 2 U.S.C. §285b, by the Office of the Law Revision Counsel of the House of Representatives. The responsibility of this office is:

> (1) To prepare, and to submit to Congress, one title at a time a complete compilation, restatement, and revision of the general and permanent laws of the United States which conforms to the understood policy, intent, and purpose of the Congress in the original enactment, with such amendments and corrections as will remove ambiguities, contradictions, and other imperfections both of substance and of form, separately stated, with a view to the enactment of each title as positive law on a title by title basis. . . .
>
> (3) To prepare and publish periodically a new edition of the United States Code (including those titles which are not yet enacted into positive law as well as those titles which have been so enacted), with annual cumulative supplements reflecting newly enacted laws.
>
> (4) To classify newly enacted provisions of law to their proper positions in the code where titles involved have not yet been enacted into positive law.
>
> (5) To prepare and submit periodically such revisions in the titles of the code which have been enacted into positive law as may be necessary to keep such titles current.

The process the codifiers follow is to choose subject titles, arrange the statutes under these titles, remove statutes or provisions that have been repealed or amended, and generally clean up confusion without varying from congressional policy, intent, or purpose. Such codification also requires a renumbering of included statutes or provisions. For example, the sections of the National Voter Registration Act of 1993 are found in 42 U.S.C. §§1973gg–1973gg-10. The titles are then individually submitted to the House Judiciary Committee to begin the enactment process. As of 1990, Congress had adopted 22 of the original 50 titles. No new title has been adopted since this time. One important reason for this "lag" is the political nature of Congress or of any legislative body. To ask legislators to enact a code is to ask them to affirm, or be accountable for, the work of past legislatures. Such an action could not be taken in a vacuum. No interested legislator or group would simply enact a code of existing law without considering the substantive and political merits of that law. This means that, from a legislative perspective, a bill to enact an unenacted code may be treated no differently than any other bill: competing for attention and subject to current political and policy views.

Many important provisions of a statute may not be codified. Provisions setting forth the statute's purposes or findings, its effective date, and its severability or nonseverability are usually omitted from the codes (but found in their notes). Provisions such as the last two just named address the effectiveness or operation of the statute but not its substance and therefore are usually omitted. Provisions setting forth legislative findings or purposes, while adding a unique meaning to a particular statute, are not codified because they are particular to the individual statute, not to the body of law as a whole. On the occasion that a code is enacted, a purpose section sometimes is included in the enacted code. This is particularly true when the enacted code is not simply the codification of existing law but a legislative attempt to enact a new statute to replace all of the existing law, for example, the Bankruptcy Act of 1994.

To the unaware, this treatment of such provisions by codifiers can sometimes be problematic. Recall the case of Giuliani v. Hevesi, discussed in Chapter Two, page 96, and Chapter Four, page 165. In a draft brief for Comptroller Hevesi, the findings and purposes clause referred to on page 165 was treated as external evidence of legislative meaning — as a part of the statute's legislative history, not as part of the statute. This occurred because this section of the statute was found in the code's footnotes. The attorneys did not understand that it was part of the enacted statute. This made a considerable difference in the presentation of the case and in its outcome. Once enacted, the purpose provision was part of the statute under consideration, rather than, at best, external evidence of the statute's meaning. Researchers could have avoided this confusion by checking the statute in the state's session laws, cross-references to which are found in all codes. Such a step should be a regular part of legislative research, particularly, as discussed in section E, because in many instances session laws and not codes are better, if not the best, evidence of the law.

E.   EVIDENCE OF THE LAW — OF CODES, SLIP LAWS, ENROLLED BILLS, AND JOURNAL ENTRIES

A statute, as described earlier, is the product of the legislative enactment process. A code is the systematic collection of statutes by subject matter. For the most part, codes, are unenacted. Such codes are, at most, prima facie evidence of the law, but not conclusive evidence of the law. This point, although rarely considered by most students of the law, should be evident. The work of the codifiers in creating and maintaining a code requires judgment concerning the impact of subsequent statutes on prior ones. Errors are sometimes made in the reading and transcribing of slip law sections or in the exercise of judgment about the applicability of particular statutes. Unenacted codes are simply the opinion of codifiers, whether public or private, as to the effect a subsequent statute has had on an earlier one. For example, did it repeal or amend an earlier decision? That is why Title 1, §204 of the United States Code provides:

> (a) **United States Code**. — The matter set forth in the edition of the Code of Laws of the United States current at any time shall, together with the then current supplement, if any, establish <u>prima facie</u> [emphasis added] the laws of the United States, general and permanent in their nature, in force on the day preceding the commencement of the session following the last session the legislation of which is included: *Provided, however*, That whenever titles of such Code shall have been enacted into positive law the text thereof shall be legal evidence of the laws therein contained, in all the courts of the United States, the several States, and the Territories and insular possessions of the United States.

Incidentally, Title 1 of the United States Code is one of the titles enacted into positive law. It was so enacted in 1947 by Public Law No. 61-278, entitled "An Act to codify and enact into positive law, Title 1 of the United States Code, entitled 'General Provisions.'"

The significance of the prima facie evidentiary status of an unenacted code provision is illustrated by a relatively recent Supreme Court decision involving the same regulatory scheme about banks and the sale of insurance used as an example on page 179. In National Bank of Oregon v. Insurance Agents, 508 U.S. 439 (1993), the issue was whether a national bank with a branch in a small community through which it sold insurance could sell insurance outside of that community. The answer to the question hinged on whether Congress had repealed the statute on which the bank claimed authority was based. The Statutes at Large contained a 1916 statute that authorized such sales of insurance by banks (39 Stat. 753), and this statute was codified in Title 12 (unenacted) of the United States Code as §92, until 1952. In 1952, the codifiers removed §92 with an explanatory note that this section had been repealed by a 1918 statute. In attempting to unravel the complicated history that led to the codifiers' decision, the Court wrote:

> Though the appearance of a provision in the current edition of the United States Code is "prima facie" evidence that the provision has the force of laws, 1 U.S.C. §204(a), it is the Statutes at Large that provides the legal evidence of laws, 1 U.S.C. §112, and despite its omission from the Code section 92 remains on the books if the Statutes at Large so dictate.

Id. at 448. United States Code §112 provides that "The United States Statutes at Large shall be legal evidence of laws . . . in all courts of the United States, the several states, and the territories and insular possessions of the United States." Similar provisions are found in state statutes.

Despite the above statutes, questions still arise as to the evidentiary conclusiveness of a slip law or enrolled bill. Sometimes in the enrollment process errors occur that result in differences between the bill enacted by the legislature and the bill presented to the executive. See, for example, Harris v. Shanahan, discussed in Chapter One, page 19. Such errors raise constitutional questions about the validity of the statute. In Field v. Clark, 143 U.S. 649 (1891), importers of various cloth materials challenged a tariff act that impacted their business. They claimed that the act was constitutionally a nullity because "a section of the bill, as it finally passed, was not in the bill authenticated by the signatures of the presiding officers of the respective houses of Congress, and approved by the President." Id. at 669. In other words, the appellant argued that the enrolled bill was, in fact, not passed by Congress. The evidence they offered to support this view comprised of entries from legislative journals and committee reports. In rendering its decision in favor of the tariff acts, the Court announced what is known as the *enrolled bill rule*:

In regard to certain matters, the Constitution expressly requires that they shall be entered on the journal. To what extent the validity of legislative action may be affected by the failure to have those matters entered on the journal, we need not inquire. No such question is presented for determination. But it is clear that, in respect to the particular mode in which, or with what fullness, shall be kept the proceedings of either house relating to matters not expressly required to be entered on the journals; whether bills, orders, resolutions, reports and amendments shall be entered at large on the journal, or only referred to and designated by their titles or by numbers; these and like matters were left to the discretion of the respective houses of Congress. Nor does any clause of that instrument, either expressly or by necessary implication, prescribe the mode in which the fact of the original passage of a bill by the House of Representatives and the Senate shall be authenticated, or preclude Congress from adopting any mode to that end which its wisdom suggests. . . .

The signing by the Speaker of the House of Representatives, and by the President of the Senate, in open session, of an enrolled bill, is an official attestation by the two houses of such bill as one that has passed Congress. It is a declaration by the two houses, through their presiding officers, to the President, that a bill, thus attested, has received, in due form, the sanction of the legislative branch of the government, and that it is delivered to him in obedience to the constitutional requirement that all bills which pass Congress shall be presented to him. And when a bill, thus attested, receives his approval, and is deposited in the public archives, its authentication as a bill that has passed Congress should be deemed complete and unimpeachable. . . .

It is admitted that an enrolled act, thus authenticated, is sufficient evidence of itself — nothing to the contrary appearing upon its face — that it passed Congress. But the contention is, that it cannot be regarded as a law of the United States if the journal of either house fails to show that it passed in the precise form in which it was signed by the presiding officers of the two houses, and approved by the President. It is said that, under any other view, it becomes possible for the Speaker of the

House of Representatives and the President of the Senate to impose upon the people as a law a bill that was never passed by Congress. But this possibility is too remote to be seriously considered in the present inquiry. It suggests a deliberate conspiracy. . . . Judicial action based upon such a suggestion is forbidden by the respect due to a coordinate branch of the government. The evils that may result from the recognition of the principle that an enrolled act, in the custody of the Secretary of State, attested by the signatures of the presiding officers of the two houses of Congress, and the approval of the President, is conclusive evidence that it was passed by Congress, according to the forms of the Constitution, would be far less than those that would certainly result from a rule making the validity of Congressional enactments depend upon the manner in which the journals of the respective houses are kept by the subordinate officers charged with the duty of keeping them. . . .

Id. at 671-673.

This rule is not universally followed. A number of states have rules that allow references, in certain instances, to legislative journals and sometimes other documents to contradict the enrolled bill as evidenced by the slip or session law. These rules effectively make the slip law or session law presumptive, not conclusive, evidence of the law, notwithstanding state statutes declaring session laws conclusive. For example, in Harris v. Shanahan, described in Chapter One, page 19, the enrolling clerk omitted from an enrolled bill a provision that had been included in the bill that had passed the legislature. The court impeached the enrolled bill on the basis of legislative journals, after stating the general rule that an enrolled bill can only be impeached if truthful legislative journals show beyond all doubt that the bill enrolled and signed by the governor was not the bill passed by the legislature.

The jurisprudence on such rules is too varied to be easily catalogued. As the reporters for the National Conference of State Legislatures have observed:

1. There does not appear to be agreement between the states concerning whether to rely on the journal record or the enrolled bill record to determine whether a bill has been duly passed and what the provisions of the bill are when there are conflicts in the records.

2. It appears that the enrolled bill as certified on the bill itself by the presiding officers and the legislative officers of both
houses is more likely to be correct than the record maintained
by the journal clerk. The state constitutions contain provisions
concerning the journal and the records that must be kept and
some have rules concerning the enrollment of bills. These
requirements vary widely from state to state. It is sometimes
difficult to reconcile the different rules for even one state and
apparently impossible to reconcile law on the subject generally.
It appears that the law in each state must be arrived at from a
consideration of the constitution, court decisions and rules of
that state.

National Conference of State Legislatures, Mason's Manual of
Legislative Procedure 481 (1989).

A word about legislative journals. In Chapter Two, we referred to the accessibility to the legislative process as one of its
legitimizing characteristics. One aspect of accessibility is the
constitutionally required maintenance by Congress and state
(and many local) legislatures of journals of their proceedings.
Journals are intended to provide public notice of the official
activities of legislative bodies and their votes. Justice Story
makes this point in writing about the federal provision:

> [T]he object of the whole clause is to insure publicity to the pro-
> ceedings of the legislature, and a correspondent responsibility
> of the members to their respective constituents. And it is
> founded in sound policy and deep political foresight. Intrigue
> and cabal are thus deprived of some of their main resources, by
> plotting and devising measures in secrecy. The public mind is
> enlightened by an attentive examination of the public measures;
> patriotism, and integrity, and wisdom obtain their due reward;
> and votes are ascertained, not by vague conjecture, but by
> positive facts. . . . So long as known and open responsibility is
> valuable as a check or an incentive among the representatives of
> a free people, so long as a journal of their proceedings and their
> votes, published in the face of the world, will continue to enjoy
> public favor and be demanded by public opinion.

Joseph Story, Constitution §§840, 841.

Article I, §5 of the Constitution requires that "[e]ach house
shall keep a journal of its proceedings, and from time to time
publish the same, excepting such parts as may, in their judg-

ment, require secrecy; and the yeas and nays of the members of either house on any question, shall at the desire of one-fifth of those present, be entered on the journal." The term *proceedings* refers to the business before the houses (for example, consideration of motions, resolutions, and bills) but does not include the debate or comments on such business. Debate and comments of members of Congress are part of the Congressional Record, which is discussed in Chapter Three, section B.

State constitutional provisions contain similar requirements, although differing sometimes on the issues of publication (for example, Alabama requires its journal to be published immediately after the adjournment of each legislative session, Ala. Const. art. IV, §55) and on the number of members necessary to have individual votes recorded (for example, Pennsylvania requires a roll call vote if two members of any house call for it, Pa. Const. art. 2, §12). Also, some states permit comments in their journals in the form of dissents or protests against specific acts or resolutions to be recorded (for example, Ala. Const. art. IV, §55; Kan. Const. art 2, §10).

Conclusion

Each year this nation's multitude of legislatures enact many thousands of new laws and consider even more ideas for legislation. As a consequence of all this legislative activity, courts throughout the country struggle daily to determine how statutes apply to particular fact patterns. These statutes and the processes through which they are enacted and interpreted demark our present legal landscape. In this age of statutes, no student of the law can comfortably study law or serve a client without knowing how statutes are enacted or interpreted. In this book, we have attempted to provide an overview of how statutory law is made and interpreted and of the characteristics intended to provide legitimacy to the legislative and interpretive processes. Our goal has been to provide an introductory and reference text, not to provide the level of detail found in a treatise on the legislative process or on statutory interpretation.

Finally, while, as part of our expository effort, we offer many criticisms of the imperfections of these processes, we acknowledge our admiration for the legislative process and for those who participate in it. What we said in the introduction to our previous book is applicable here as well: "We hope that by writing this book we share an informed enthusiasm with teachers and students and spur some of them to direct engagement with the processes and its needed reforms." Abner J. Mikva and Eric Lane, Legislative Process xxiv (1995).

Table of Authorities

Alexander, Herbert E., Financing Politics (3d ed. 1984), 74

Bach, Stanley, The Nature of Congressional Rules, 5 Journal of Law & Politics 725 (1989), 97, 98
Bach, S. & S. S. Smith, Managing Uncertainty in the House of Representatives (1988), 129
Blatt, William S., The History of Statutory Interpretation: A Study in Form and Substance, 6 Cardozo L. Rev. 799 (1985), 5
Bonfield, Arthur E. & Michael Asimow, State and Federal Administrative Law (1989), 50
Breyer, Stephen, On the Uses of Legislative History in Interpreting Statutes, 65 S. Cal. L. Rev. 845 (1992), 29, 54
Byrd, Sen. Robert C., N.Y. Times, April 4, 1990, 73

Cardozo, Benjamin N., The Nature of the Judicial Process (1921), 42
Cigler, Allan J. & Burdett A. Loomis, Introduction, Interest Group Politics (3d ed. 1991), 79, 81
Congressional Quarterly, Guide to Congress (4th ed. 1991), 103
Correia, Edward O., A Legislative Conception of Legislative Supremacy, 42 Case W. Res. L. Rev. 1129 (1992), 36
Costello, George A., Average Voting Members and Other "Benign Fictions": The Relative Reliability of Committee Reports, Floor Debates, and Other Sources of Legislative History, 1990 Duke L.J. 39, 36

Dickerson, Reed, The Fundamentals of Legal Drafting (1965), 152
Dickerson, Reed, The Interpretation and Application of Statutes (1975), 35
Dorgan, Rep. Byron, N.Y. Times, March 31, 1990, 73

Easterbrook, Frank H., Statutes' Domain, 50 U. Chi. L. Rev. 533 (1983), 51
Eskridge, William N., Dynamic Statutory Interpretation, 135 U. Pa. L. Rev. 1479 (1987), 53
Eskridge, William N. & Phillip P. Frickey, Cases and Materials on Legislation (1988), 25

Rudd, Millard H., No Law Shall Embrace More Than One Subject, 42 Minn.
    L. Rev. 389 (1958), 163, 164

Schacter, Jane S., The Pursuit of "Popular Intent": Interpretive Dilemmas in
    Direct Democracy, 105 Yale L.J. 107 (1995), 56
Schoenbrod, David, Power without Responsibility, How Congress Abuses
    the People through Delegation (1993), 49
Starr, Kenneth W., Observations About The Use of Legislative History, 1987
    Duke L.J. 371 (1987), 30
Strauss, Peter, When the Judge Is Not the Primary Official with
    Responsibility to Read: Agency Interpretation and the Problem of
    Legislative History, 66 Chi.-Kent L. Rev. 321 (1990), 49
Story, Joseph, Constitution, 186
Sunstein, Cass R., After the Rights Revolution (1990), 4
Sunstein, Cass R., Interpreting Statutes in the Regulatory State, 103 Harv. L.
    Rev. 405 (1989), 48, 51
Susman, Thomas M. & ABA Section of Administrative Law and Regulatory
    Practice, Lobbying Manual, Chap. 8 (1993), 83

Tiefer, Charles, Congressional Practice and Procedure (1989), 91, 129

Wald, Patricia M., The Sizzling Sleeper: The Use of Legislative History in
    Construing Statutes in the 1988-89 Term of the United States Supreme
    Court, 39 Am. U. L. Rev. 277 (1990), 5, 34
Wald, Patricia M., Some Observations on the Use of Legislative History in
    the 1981 Supreme Court Term, 68 Iowa L. Rev. 195 (1983), 30

Williams, Robert F., State Constitutional Limits on Legislative Procedure:
    Legislative Compliance and Judicial Enforcement, 48 U. Pitt. L. Rev.
    797 (1987), 98-99
Wilson, Woodrow, Congressional Government (John Hopkins Univ. Press
    ed. 1981), 60, 139
Wood, Gordon, The Creation of the American Republic, 1776-1787 (1969), 72

Table of Cases

Table of Statutes

Index